RHNS *Averof*

RHNS *Averof*

Thunder in the Aegean

John C. Carr

Pen & Sword
MARITIME

First published in Great Britain in 2014 by
Pen & Sword Maritime
an imprint of
Pen & Sword Books Ltd
47 Church Street
Barnsley
South Yorkshire
S70 2AS

Copyright © John C. Carr 2014

ISBN 978 1 78303 021 7

Typeset in Ehrhardt by
Mac Style Ltd, Bridlington, East Yorkshire
Printed and bound in the UK by CPI Group (UK) Ltd,
Croydon, CRO 4YY

Pen & Sword Books Ltd incorporates the imprints of Pen &
Sword Archaeology, Atlas, Aviation, Battleground, Discovery,
Family History, History, Maritime, Military, Naval, Politics,
Railways, Select, Transport, True Crime, and Fiction, Frontline
Books, Leo Cooper, Praetorian Press, Seaforth Publishing and
Wharncliffe.

For a complete list of Pen & Sword titles please contact
PEN & SWORD BOOKS LIMITED
47 Church Street, Barnsley, South Yorkshire, S70 2AS, England
E-mail: enquiries@pen-and-sword.co.uk
Website: www.pen-and-sword.co.uk

Contents

Prologue

*If you consider how many times the Averof escaped disaster,
you have to agree that the ship was blessed by God.*
        Leading Seaman (later Sub Lieutenant) George Gousis

I n a compartment on the port side of RHNS *Averof* there's an old
tin bucket standing upside down on a table. The bucket is one of
the many exhibits in the venerable armoured cruiser – 102 years
old at this writing – which is enjoying an honourable retirement as a
floating museum. A guide points to what looks like a calcium deposit
stain on the side of the bucket just below the handle. Look closer,
and the stain resolves itself into a tiny face a couple of inches wide –
rudimentary eyes and mouth and short beard, surrounded by what
looks very like a halo.

The stain has been there for almost as long as the ship itself. It
was first noticed by a crewmember on 20 November 1912, when the
Averof was steaming towards a decisive encounter with the Turkish
fleet off Cape Helles at the entrance to the Dardanelles. One officer
saw in it the image of Saint Nicholas, the Greeks' patron saint of
the sea and seafarers, and forecast – correctly, as it turned out – that
the ship would emerge victorious from the coming encounter with
minimum casualties.

From that day on, the powder bucket was taken into the ship's
tiny chapel as a sacred relic. A good many people today are quite

prepared to believe that some sort of supernatural guidance helped preserve the *Averof* through decades of war and neglect. Whatever one believes, it's an undoubted fact that the way the *Averof* has emerged largely unscathed from a century of ordeals which would have sunk any ordinary vessel many times over, and to survive into the twenty-first century as a venerated veteran of Greece's wars at sea, is something of a miracle in itself.

My first acquaintance with RHNS *Averof* came during my first Greek island holiday at the age of thirteen. Standing at the rail of an island-hopping passenger boat, drinking in that wonderful Greek sunshine, I caught sight of its long grey hull moored at the resort island of Poros and remember that it seemed oddly out of place among the put-putting caiques and small white ships filling the Poros channel. It was obviously a relic of another age.

It was a time when Greece was getting on with the peaceful business of building up tourism, and so it is no surprise that the *Averof* was bypassed by galloping modernity. Only later, when I began a career in journalism, did I get the urge to find out more about that silent hulking presence outside the Naval Petty Officers' School at Poros. It was as late as 1984, when the ship was towed from Poros to become a floating museum in Phaleron Bay, within easy distance of the city of Athens, that the public at large were made aware of what the RHNS *Averof* (or *Georgios Averof*, to give it its official but rarely used full name) had contributed to modern Greek statehood. For in 1913 it had literally been the ship that won a war.

In December 2012 – the centenary, in fact, of the *Averof*'s greatest sea battle, almost to the day – my editor at Pen and Sword, Philip Sidnell, gave me the green light for this book while we were sipping coffee in Saint Pancras station in London. I had just completed the draft of my previous work, *The Defence and Fall of Greece 1940–1941*, and found myself with a large amount of unused research material in Greek, especially in the naval sector, which could really use a dedicated English-language readership. This, combined with the fact that the *Averof* is the world's oldest surviving pre-dreadnought armoured cruiser still afloat and an active maritime museum wallowing in the warm Saronic Gulf alongside bevies of luxury yachts, argued strongly for a serious history of the vessel in English.

Writing this book was an education for me, as I had always considered myself an aviation specialist in military history. I am by no means a happy sailor, and couldn't tell a swabbed deck from a forestay. I'm glad that this book gave me the opportunity to expand my military knowledge into matters maritime, though I'm tempted to repeat the caveat of Lemuel Gulliver's fictional publisher that 'my own ignorance in sea-affairs shall have led me to commit some mistakes'.[1] If the naval reader does note such mistakes, I beg a landlubber forgiveness.

As the *Averof* (correct pronunciation: Av-AIR-off) was most active during the Balkan Wars of 1912–13, I have found it necessary, of course, to fill in some details and history of Greece's adversary, the Ottoman Empire, which was in its dying days. The Ottoman Turkish navy had fallen a long way since its glory days of the sixteenth century when it all but ruled the Mediterranean. Yet in the years before the First World War it could field powerful pre-dreadnought warships against which the *Averof* would prove its mettle in the Aegean Sea.

To remove possible sources of confusion for the reader, I must include a note on Turkish usage. Regarding references to military officers with names such as Enver Bey and Shevket Pasha, the terms 'Bey' and 'Pasha' were not surnames but titles, roughly corresponding to 'Sir' and 'General'. The Turks did not employ surnames on the Western model until 1935, well after the Kemalist revolution. However, where my sources list Ottoman-era equivalents to surnames, I use them. In spelling I have resisted the pedantic temptation to retain obscure Turkish orthographical features such as the undotted i (ı) or thick sh (ş) as they might confuse and perhaps annoy the non-linguist (thus the more familiar Pasha instead of *Paşa*), but have kept the umlauted ü (as in Abdülhamid) as having no phonetic equivalent in English.

I have decided not to burden a book of this modest length with numbered references in the text, apart from the occasional footnote. I list my sources in a bibliographical note at the end, with a few comments about each. As regards those who helped me get the material for this book together, first and foremost I must thank fellow-author Alex Martin for setting me upon the naval trail in the first place. Dimitris Pitellos, a shipping executive and naval enthusiast, has been of inestimable value in unearthing priceless source material on his own initiative. A great debt, as always, is owed to George Mermingas for his seemingly inexhaustible library on all aspects of Greek military history, and Vice Admiral (ret.) Ioannis Paloumbis, the curator of the Hellenic Maritime Museum, for his eager and friendly cooperation in securing historic photographs. The museum librarian, Katia Kraniotou, was especially helpful in tracking down old technical documents. Yannis Korodimos, the public relations director of the Hellenic War Museum, was always on hand with his support, while Able Seaman Markos Christodoulidis, a guide and crewmember of the *Averof,* has conducted me several times through its quarters and engine room, offering fascinating glimpses into history and legend.

John C Carr
Athens
April 2013

List of Illustrations

Credits:

Hellenic Maritime Museum: Nos. 1–5, 7–17, 52–3.

Nike Morgan: Nos. 6, 18, 20–1, 44, 50.

Author: Nos. 15, 19, 22–49, 51, 55.

List of Maps

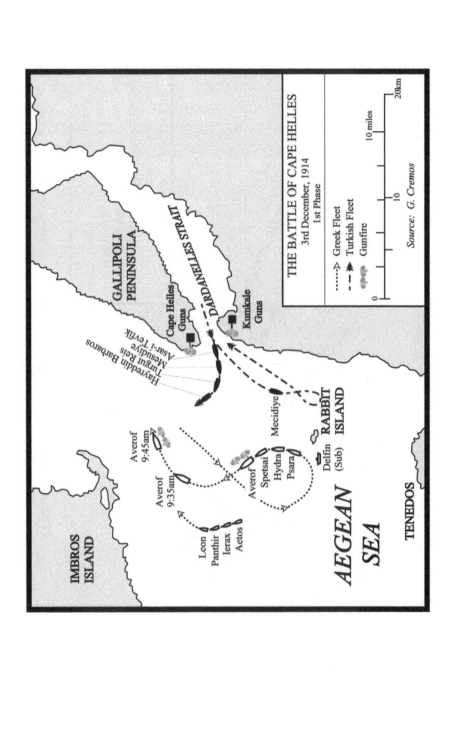

IMBROS
ISLAND

GALLIPOLI
PENINSULA

DARDANELLES STRAIT

Cape Helles
Guns

Asar-1 Tevfik
Mesudiye
Turgut Reis
Hayreddin Barbaros

Kumkale
Guns

Averof
9:45am

Averof
9:35am

Leon
Panthir
Ierax
Aetos

Averof
Spetsai
Hydra
Psara

Mecidiye

RABBIT
ISLAND

Delfin
(Sub)

AEGEAN
SEA

TENEDOS

THE BATTLE OF CAPE HELLES
3rd December, 1914
1st Phase

·····▷ Greek Fleet
- - -➤ Turkish Fleet
        Gunfire

0   10   20km

0   10 miles

Source: G. Cremos

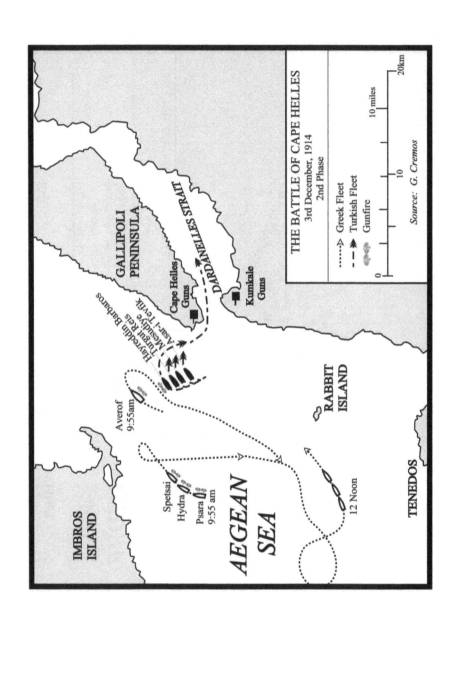

THE BATTLE OF CAPE HELLES
3rd December, 1914
2nd Phase

Source: G. Cremos

Greek Fleet
Turkish Fleet
Gunfire

10 miles
20km

IMBROS ISLAND

GALLIPOLI PENINSULA

DARDANELLES STRAIT

Cape Helles Guns

Kumkale Guns

Hayreddin Barbaros
Turgut Reis
Mesudiye
Asar-i Tevfik

Averof 9:55am

Spetsai
Hydra
Psara 9:55 am

AEGEAN SEA

RABBIT ISLAND

12 Noon

TENEDOS

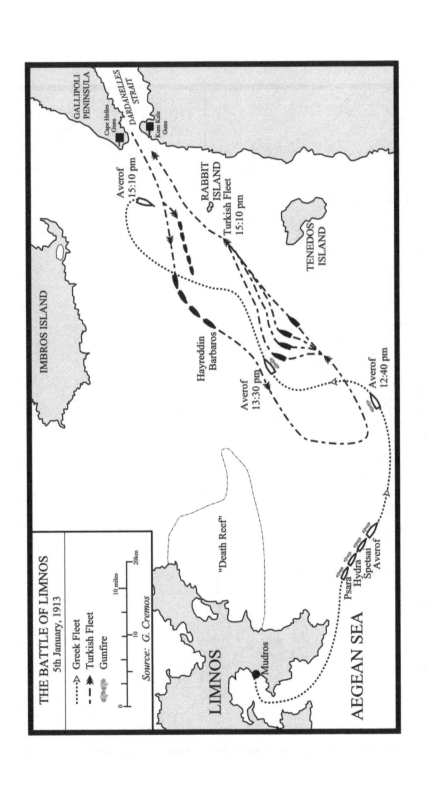

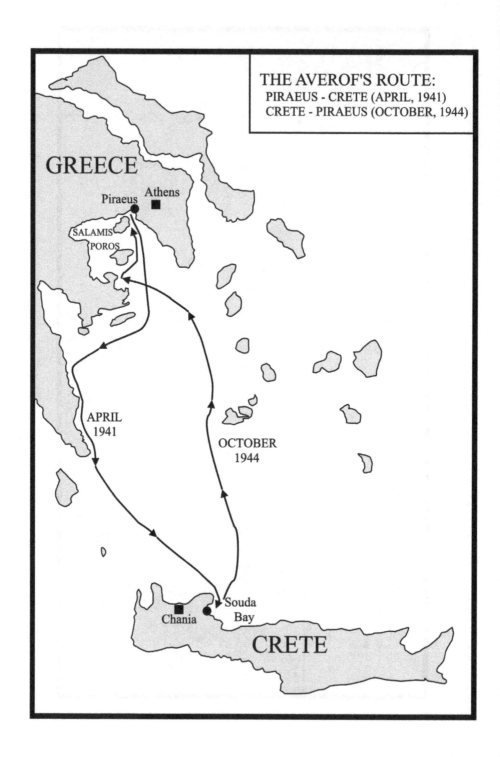

THE AVEROF'S ROUTE:
PIRAEUS - CRETE (APRIL, 1941)
CRETE - PIRAEUS (OCTOBER, 1944)

GREECE

Piraeus Athens

SALAMIS
POROS

APRIL
1941

OCTOBER
1944

Souda
Bay

Chania

CRETE

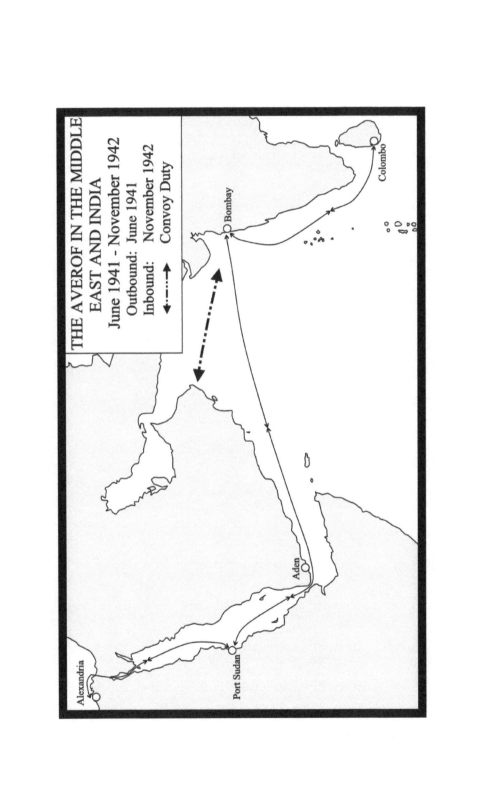

THE AVEROF IN THE MIDDLE
EAST AND INDIA
June 1941 - November 1942
Outbound: June 1941
Inbound: November 1942
Convoy Duty

Colombo

Bombay

Aden

Port Sudan

Alexandria

Chapter 1

Rush Job

They called him Mr Zedzed. That was just one of the unflattering sobriquets belonging to Basil Zaharoff, also known to his many detractors as Merchant of Death and High Priest of War. Not that he really minded. In his chequered career he found he was astoundingly good at one thing, and that was arms dealing and making large amounts of money out of it. Zaharoff was the epitome of the realist businessman who knows human nature for what it is, and trades without scruples on its more bestial elements. His own views on war mattered little. He was personally as powerless to stop nations from slaughtering one another as was a conscripted milkman in uniform. Yet he knew there was big money to be made out of that ineradicable human failing, and as long as the demand was there, why not meet it? Zaharoff also took full advantage of another quirk of human nature – the tendency of the powers-that-be to woo sinister arms merchants and grant them automatic entrée into the highest circles of society. In the early years of the twentieth century, British high society fulfilled that role for him quite amply.

Born to a Greek family in Turkey as Vasilios Zacharias, he had Russified his name to give it more of an exotic and slightly menacing cachet, and thus glided grandly and awesomely in exalted circles as Basil Zaharoff, his very name by now a synonym for the guns and shells and ships he sold to insecure kings and presidents and prime ministers. In 1910 Zaharoff was around 60 years old, a distinguished and meticulously cut grey beard topping his silken cravat and pearl cravat-pin. Much of his long and complex career before that date remains a mystery. He spent a brief period of his youth in Odessa where he had altered his name. His foes claimed he began his first business venture drumming up custom for a brothel in Constantinople, moving on to cleverer things such as setting fire to large mansions in order to get kickbacks from the Constantinople Fire Department – and rewards from the grateful but unwitting owners whose valuables he would, of course, take care to rescue first. Hostile accounts detail all manner of nefarious works all the way up to the outbreak of the First World War – which many, not surprisingly, accused him of actually bringing about, as by then his reputation as a global 'death merchant' was well and truly established. Doors opened everywhere. British and Continental nobility negotiated on familiar terms with Mr Zedzed, who basked in the notoriety and secretly enjoyed seeing the rich and powerful at his feet.

That was about the time the British writer Osbert Sitwell famously described Basil Zaharoff's 'beaky face, hooded eye … the impression of sheer power and the capacity to wait'. Zaharoff had been in Britain on and off since about 1870, marrying a girl from Bristol but upsetting his domestic bliss by getting arrested for embezzlement. In the 1870s the major powers of Europe were setting out on a merciless arms race, and Zaharoff at some point tapped into what would make his fortune by becoming the Balkan sales agent for the Swedish firm of Thorsten Nordenfelt, which at the time was experimenting with the production of submarines. That way he came into contact with Sir Hiram Maxim, the inventor of the Maxim machine gun. By 1897, when the munitions firm of Vickers merged with Maxim-Nordenfelt, Zaharoff had become the firm's chief overseas salesman, earning huge commissions. Thanks to his creative sales techniques, which included bribery on a grand scale, Vickers found itself arming Russia, Turkey and Greece, to name just the three powers with which he had personal connections, with state-of-the-art submarines and Maxim guns. So when the Greek government in 1912 found it needed a rather large quantity of naval shells and cordite charges for an impending clash with Turkey in the Aegean Sea, and Britain baulked at supplying them so as not to ignite a clash in the eastern Mediterranean, the services of the 'wickedest man in the world' were secretly sought.[1]

Mr Zedzed seems to have had no known political ideology. Yet the evidence suggests that he had one emotional soft spot (albeit well concealed), and that was for his ethnic homeland Greece. It would have been entirely understandable for him to believe that Greece should become a power to be reckoned with in the Mediterranean. Having grown up in the Ottoman heartland, he would have been well versed in the Greeks' long-standing desire for independence from Turkish rule. In 1912 Greece had been an independent nation for eighty-three years. Yet millions of ethnic Greeks still lived in large swathes of territory controlled by the Ottoman Empire in the Balkans and Asia Minor. A main tenet of Greek foreign policy throughout the late nineteenth century, driven by an aggressively chauvinist media, was to 'liberate' those areas from the alien Turks and bring them into the Greek fold. As the Ottoman Empire began decaying, this Greek irredentism became stronger in proportion, especially as it attracted the sympathy and support of the educated classes in most of Western Europe. Partly in response to growing public sentiment, Greek governments had been giving increasing thought to beefing up the navy. Greece was thus, thanks to Zaharoff, one of the first European nations to acquire a Nordenfelt submarine in the late 1880s – one of just six that were produced.

In 1912 Greece, Bulgaria and Serbia joined forces to expel the Turks from the Balkans and enlarge their own borders in the process. Athens was especially concerned about the Aegean Sea, where the Ottoman Empire was holding on to the ethnically-Greek islands of Limnos, Lesvos, Chios and Samos off the Turkish coast, as well as the Dodecanese islands farther south, and Greek policy was to wrest them away. The pride of the Royal Hellenic Navy was the 10,000-ton armoured cruiser RHNS *Averof,* launched from the Orlando shipyard at Livorno (Leghorn) the previous year. Though not quite the last word in naval hardware, the cruiser was ideal for Greece's needs. Barely had the *Averof* finished its sea trials than it had been rushed into the First Balkan War, and by November 1912 was anchored in Mudros Bay at Limnos awaiting battle with the Turkish fleet. But such was the haste with which the cruiser had been despatched that the fleet commander whose flagship the *Averof* was, Rear Admiral Pavlos Koundouriotis, had at his disposal no more than twenty-five rounds of ammunition per gun turret – whatever could be saved from gunnery trials. More shells were needed, and fast.

The record here becomes very vague. There have been unproven allegations that both Vickers and Zaharoff were holding out for a higher price, hence the delay in delivery. More likely, the British government was queasy about supplying arms to belligerents (and unwilling to antagonize the Ottoman Empire even at that late date). It is not hard to imagine Zaharoff having a quiet word with his bosses at Vickers and perhaps oiling the unseen transaction with some of his own largesse. Whatever the truth, one rainy night a Greek freighter sidled up to a remote jetty on the Thames estuary and loaded the required shells and powder charges in complete secrecy. Continuing bad weather, however, forced the freighter to shelter at Falmouth Roads, considerably risking discovery and arrest. A month later the ship sailed into Piraeus, its precious cargo finally catching up with the *Averof* at Mudros Bay in mid-November.

Despite our near-total lack of knowledge of how the transfer was carried out, the available evidence argues strongly for Zaharoff's key involvement. The details may well have been among the vast files, including fifty-eight years of diary entries, which he flung into the fireplace of his Paris mansion in 1927. That was nearly a decade after a grateful David Lloyd George, the British prime minister, had talked King George V into figuratively (and grudgingly) laying the sword on the well-tailored shoulders of the Greek tycoon, dubbing him Sir Basil Zaharoff for his services to the British war effort. After Sir Basil's death in 1936, his servants burned more 'tons of documents' that certainly would have thrown light on how he came to have a net worth of some $1.2 billion made during the First World War, as was widely reported in the newspapers at the time.[2]

It would be tempting to assume that Greece's acquisition of one of the most modern large warships of the time, given the Athens government's chronic financial straits, owed a great deal to Zaharoff's covert oiling of the wheels. The destruction of his files, of course, limits us to mere speculation. Yet he certainly must have looked with pride on the great steel monster on which the blue and white flag of Greece proudly fluttered. That did not mean, of course, that he did not supply hardware to the Turks as well, especially two Nordenfelt submarines. 'Trade knows no flag,' said the Scottish-American industrialist and philanthropist Andrew Carnegie, and the same manifestly applied to Zaharoff, who was careful not to mix his business with politics. The world was, and is, far from being a community of saints. If nations and governments insisted on paying fortunes for instruments with which to kill large numbers of people, he was simply supplying the demand; if he didn't, someone else would. In economic theory, the world's commodities are divided into those for peace and those for war, symbolized respectively by butter and guns. Some merchants sold butter; Mr Zedzed elected to sell guns. That was all there was to it.

> This day will be an unforgettable one for me. Such has been the emotion and enthusiasm which I experienced that I consider myself lucky in that in our days we had the good fortune to see our brethren, enslaved for many centuries, be freed.

Thus wrote Sub Lieutenant George Katsouros, an engineer officer on the *Averof,* in his diary on 5 October 1912 when at 8.00 am the bugle sounded and the crew assembled on deck to receive the prime minister and navy minister who would announce the formal severance of diplomatic ties with Turkey and the commencement of a state of war. After a steam pinnace brought the dignitaries on board, and the ship's ornately-robed and bearded Orthodox priest-chaplain blessed the crew, the first order was read out, promoting Koundouriotis, until then a captain, to rear admiral.[3]

As Katsouros' diary indicates, there was not a man in either the Greek army or navy who wasn't suffused by the ideology of 'liberating' the Greeks from the purported 'shackles' of the Ottoman Empire. Beneath the feet of the *Averof*'s crew purred the shiny new powerful engines that would finally accomplish this feat; the massive guns casting their shadow over the deck would be the Greeks' long-awaited fiery sword to clear the Aegean of the Turk. That morning the prime minister, the capable and highly-regarded liberal Eleftherios Venizelos, addressed the assembled seamen and stoked their emotions to white heat:

> I had wanted, instead of directing the fortunes of a nation, to be either an officer, petty officer or seaman. That is why, gentlemen, I envy you. Never has Greece undergone more critical moments

... Greece will not remain small; she will become great. I hope that the war will be brief and victory ours.

Venizelos' words were a prime example of the political thinking of the time. This was the age of the climax of nationalism; the world was a jungle and a nation had to expend all its energies to become 'great'. Not so long before in history, expansion and power had fuelled domestic economic prosperity, as the British Empire had demonstrated. Now, however, expansion and power had become ends in themselves. The prevailing theory was well put by Otto von Bismarck, the towering German chancellor of the late nineteenth century, who said that as soon as an organism stops growing it begins to rot. The statesmen of Europe, including President Theodore Roosevelt of the United States, had taken those words at face value.

What was Greece getting out of this? In reply, the Greeks of the early twentieth century would point with pride to their ancient forebears. If they enjoyed a commanding presence in the world's history books, should not modern Greece also? If there was ever a time for national muscle-flexing, this was it. The crew of the *Averof* cheered Venizelos' words, tears running down their faces. Koundouriotis got in a reply to the effect that he and his crew would return from the expected showdown with the Turks 'either victors or dead' – a Spartan touch that went down well, before another launch sidled up to the *Averof*'s great hull bearing a dignified elderly gentleman with a large handlebar moustache. King George I, of Bavarian birth, had been forty-nine years on the Greek throne. Though he had not yet rid himself of his German accent, in all other respects he felt as Greek as anyone in his realm. In a brief but fervent address George I adjured his sailors to 'add another glorious page' to the long annals of Greek naval history. Half an hour after the crew's cheers subsided and king, prime minister and navy minister had departed, 'the propellers of the ships, led by the flagship *Averof*,' wrote Katsouros in his diary, 'furrowed the sea in the Bay of Phaleron, leading us to wherever the honour of the country would call.'

On the open bridge of the new armoured cruiser, steering his charge southeast around Cape Sounion and steaming into the Aegean Sea, Rear Admiral Koundouriotis felt the bracing sea breeze on his face and could well enjoy a certain pride in having achieved a new level in his family's already formidable maritime history.

The small island of Hydra (or Ydra in Greek), as many modern vacationers know, rises in a steep hump off the coast of Argolis about eighty miles southwest of Athens. Hydra is actually the top bit of a long submerged mountain. Having precious little water or vegetation, it was barely inhabited until the late eighteenth century when Albanian refugees, coming south to seek a protected haven, settled there to escape Turkish misrule. The only feasible economic activity was fishing and then, as the islanders gained in maritime experience, seaborne trade. As the picturesque little main town took shape like a quaint amphitheatre around the only practical harbour, a few families began to dominate that trade which within a few decades achieved Mediterranean-wide proportions. They certainly had plenty of business acumen. One or two families made large fortunes running the British blockade of enemy ports during the Napoleonic wars. One such family was that of Koundouriotis, which by the time the Greek revolt broke out in 1821 was able to place fifty-two armed merchantmen at the disposal of the rebels. These ships were vital in clearing the Peloponnesian coasts and some of the Aegean islands of the Ottoman Turks. The combat experience gained was important in helping establish the navy after independence. The eldest member of the family at the time, George Koundouriotis, was rewarded by being made president of the rebel government.

The Koundouriotis family became Greek only very gradually. They never forgot that they were Albanians, with more than a touch of the aggressiveness that typifies that ethnic group. George Koundouriotis, though the titular chief of the Greek rebels, could barely speak Greek himself. The family, in fact, had already become a prototype of the typical 'Greek tycoon' clan of a later age – Greek in name only, and basically cosmopolitan. Some of the Greek rebel chieftains sensed this and directed their energies more towards trying to unseat the Albanian shipowner than expelling the Turks, who launched a devastating counteroffensive in 1825. The following year, Koundouriotis' fragile administration collapsed, but not before he had taken a vital step to keep the revolt going: he had the brilliant idea of inviting a capable British soldier in the service of Naples, Sir Richard Church, to organize the Greek rebel army into a professional fighting force, and Lord Cochrane, a cashiered Royal Navy officer who had found employment in South American revolutionary combat, to do the same for the Greeks' navy. Both men – one an Irishman and the other a Scot – were familiar with the Latin and Mediterranean mentalities and thus knew how to command Greeks in the field.

As Cochrane got to work harassing Turkish vessels in the waters around the Peloponnese, another English ex-Royal Navy naval volunteer for the Greek cause, Captain Frank Hastings, was doing the same with a frigate in the confines of the Gulf of Corinth. Despite their best efforts, though, it took the Royal Navy proper to help deal the decisive blow to the Turks. It was Turkish atrocities in the Peloponnese that moved Admiral Sir Edward Codrington, the British naval commander in the Mediterranean, to defy official British policy and move against the Ottomans. The opposing fleets – including French and Russian squadrons operating with Codrington – clashed in the Bay of Navarino in October 1827, and the Turkish fleet under Ibrahim Pasha was blown to matchwood. It was that encounter, more than any other, which ensured that modern Greece would become an independent state two years later.

The contribution to history of the Koundouriotis family was by no means finished. George Koundouriotis' grandson Pavlos was born on Hydra in 1855. The latter half of the nineteenth century saw several small local revolts in parts of Greece still under Turkish control, such as Crete. Pavlos Koundouriotis, true to the combative tradition of the family, played his part in a few of them. Following in his forebears' nautical footsteps, he entered the Naval Academy at nineteen. While still a junior officer, he saw action off Preveza when his vessel bombarded the Turkish fort in that town and was lucky to escape retaliation from a force several times the size of his own. He also took part in a hazardous voyage to aid the Cretan rebels. By 1901 his naval career had developed to the point of his being appointed to command the training ship RHNS *Miaoulis* which was the first Greek naval vessel to traverse the Atlantic with a crew of cadets. He was 56 years old when, as aide-de-camp to King George I and commander of the RHN's First Naval Division, he was picked to head the Naval Academy and then command the *Averof*.

Rear Admiral Koundouriotis may or may not have known of Basil Zaharoff's machinations on behalf of Greek naval power. But he had every reason to feel relieved when he took his boxes of ammunition on board. Mudros Bay had no coaling or supply stations; everything had to be shipped in from the mainland. It was an unusually cold autumn, too, with freezing winds howling over the northern Aegean. The Dardanelles strait, from where the Turkish fleet was daily expected to emerge, was just thirty-seven miles away to the east. The Greeks, meanwhile, had landed marine detachments on Limnos, sweeping aside its small Turkish garrison, and followed up the operation with similar landings on Imvros, Samothrake, Psara, Thasos, Skiathos and the Mount Athos peninsula.

Those were just side-shows. The big prey was the Ottoman fleet. Koundouriotis knew it was there, sheltering in the strait behind the long outline of the Gallipoli peninsula. He sent destroyers to patrol the entrance to the strait to try and lure the Turks out. Lurking under the surface was the RHN submarine *Delfin*, newly delivered from France, while a Farman hydroplane appropriately named the *Nautilus* – very likely the first use of a reconnaissance aircraft in naval operations anywhere in the world – skimmed the waves. As the weather worsened, Koundouriotis was getting impatient. All of Greece was hanging on his decision. The mighty *Averof* had become the biggest source of national pride second only to the Parthenon – here at last was the steel and thunder that were the trademarks of a great European power. The ship had become an icon, its crew latter-day crusaders against the alien occupier, the Muslim power to the east. Day by day Koundouriotis scanned the watery horizon through his binoculars, and Greece waited for the chance to fire the big guns in anger and shred the red flag with the crescent on it.

Chapter 2

The Wine-Dark Sea

Gazing out at the distant, mist-shrouded green and ochre hills of the Asia Minor coast, Koundouriotis cannot have helped thinking back to the naval achievements of his countrymen in those very waters over many centuries. On the other side of that long green peninsula to the east flowed the strait of the Dardanelles, through which Greek hulls had been sailing back and forth since before the Trojan War about 1200 BC. This part of the Mediterranean, including the islands studding the Aegean Sea to the south, was the classical Greek heartland. Greek city-states had flourished on all the adjacent coasts for many hundreds of years. To defend this area – or to wrest it from alien domination – came naturally to the mind of every Greek who had ever gone to school. In the opening years of the twentieth century there were aliens occupying the eastern Greek seas and islands, and these were the Muslim Turks, ensconced there for the better part of half a millennium. The passage of so much time had only intensified the Greek desire to get the territories back. And now that the Ottoman Empire, by all accounts, was in the terminal stages of decay, it seemed as though the ghosts of Themistokles, Perikles and Alexander were rising from the waters to reassert the Greeks' primacy in their own *mare nostrum*. The shades of the ancient and mediaeval Greek mariners, who had battled Persian and Turk in these waters, would be at last avenged.

The Greeks as an ethnic group originated in what is now Ukraine, and relocated to the southern Balkans about 1900 BC. Within a short time this pastoral, sky-worshipping people had absorbed the seafaring talents of the pre-Greek inhabitants of the peninsula and taken the nautical art to new heights. By about 1500 BC great amphibious forces of Achaians (the most common name for the earliest Greeks) set out from the fortified centres of Mykenai and Pylos to raid the Asia Minor coast in search of supplies and childbearing women. The successes of these Vikings of antiquity were based on the use of troop carriers and supply ships large and strong enough to withstand long voyages and take on loads of seized booty. Much of the Achaians' seafaring knowledge was almost certainly derived from the Minoans of Crete, whose kings had maintained a powerful navy to guard their own extensive trade before being taken over by the Greeks.

When population pressures became too great in many Greek city-states, groups of young families would pile into boats to sail over the water in search of new lives, much as poor and persecuted Europeans relocated to the New World after America was discovered. The ships carrying these people – plus livestock and farming plants – had to be hardy. Greek colonies cropped up in Asia Minor and Sicily, and as far west as Massalia (Marseilles). The coasts of the Black Sea were rich in grain, which the mainland Greeks sorely needed. A great part of Greek seaborne trade thus went through the Dardanelles and Bosporus straits. This grain route was so important that it triggered more than one major war, beginning with the campaign against Troy and ending with the conquests of Alexander III of Macedon (the Great) 800 years later. The constant rivalry in the eastern Aegean was the spur for naval-minded Greeks to invent new and more efficient warships to guard the merchantmen carrying the grain on the inbound trips, and wine and olive oil for export.

The Greeks' early love of seafaring adventure is reflected in the lines of the bard Homer, whose *Iliad* and *Odyssey* are full of vivid descriptions of maritime activity. To take just one exhilarating example, in Book One of the *Iliad* a Greek crew is described setting sail for the main Greek camp at Troy:

And Apollo who works from afar sent them a favouring stern wind.
  They set up the mast again and spread on it the white sails,
  And the wind blew into the middle of the sail, and at the cutwater
  A blue wave rose and sang strongly as the ship went onward.
  She ran swiftly cutting across the swell her pathway.[1]

A passage such as this is not only a paean to gung-ho optimism. It's suffused with the very spirit of freedom. It's no historical accident that the first ideas of political liberty arose among people used to the heady freedom of seafaring, where there are no boundaries, where the horizon of clouds and islands changes every moment, where the unpredictable elements develop a ship master's talent for making snap decisions without needing to bow to or get permission from an authority. A man at sea is his own boss. Homer's frequent use of the simile 'wine-dark' to describe the sea is no mere literary device. The sea's freedom can make one drunk. No experience like the seagoing experience leaves such a libertarian mark on the character. Thus it was that the ancient Athenians, who survived largely by trade across the Aegean Sea, instituted the world's first workable model of democracy at the end of the sixth century BC. And they, along with the commercial city of Corinth, were the first to adopt advanced ideas of shipbuilding from the Phoenicians at the eastern end of the Mediterranean. Good warships were the best protection for trade – a paradigm that Britain's Royal Navy would follow in the eighteenth and nineteenth centuries and the United States Navy in the twentieth.

It was the Corinthians, in fact, who developed the first European warship *per se*, that is, designed not only for carrying men and supplies, but as a fighting machine in its own right, equipped with armaments such as a prow ram whose purpose was to destroy the enemy vessel itself as distinct from dealing with the enemy soldiers on board. The Corinthian fifty-oared pentekonter proved its worth in the first recorded purely naval battle in Europe, the showdown between the fleets of Corinth and its old colony Korkyra in 664 BC. Greek cities in the Aegean area were also building war fleets at that time. As their purpose became more specialized, warships began to differ in design from the old transports; they became slimmer and more streamlined in order to slice through the water, and depended on the muscle power of oarsmen for greater manoeuvrability in combat. Sails were hoisted only when the winds were favourable and the crews needed a rest.

A typical Corinthian pentekonter had port and starboard decks inside the hull from which marines could jump on enemy vessels alongside. But its main advantage soon proved to be its ram, fixed to the prow and buttressed by beams connected to the ship sides. The use of the ram, in turn, affected tactics and training. To ram an enemy vessel broadside required a high degree of oarsmanship and discipline to get the attacking ship into position with minimum delay; the ship itself, correspondingly, had to be light and easily manoeuvrable. A lighter ship could take on more oarsmen and slim down the complement of marines. Further design improvements included reducing the freeboard – and visibility to the enemy – and eliminating extra superstructure. The pentekonters of the Greek maritime states held the Aegean area together.

Just before the turn of the fifth century BC a new class of warship began to phase out the pentekonter. This was the trireme (*trieres*), the first of the truly great warships of the ancient world. The design of the trireme probably originated in Samos, an eastern Aegean island state that operated a formidable navy. The Corinthians soon caught on, and one of their shipwrights, named as Ameinokles, is believed to have built the first types on the mainland. As its name indicated, the trireme had three rows of oars on each side, totalling 170, but arranged in such a way as to have a free scope for motion without getting in one another's way. Lower and sleeker than the pentekonter, the trireme was built for lightness and speed rather than strength. Its bronze-clad prow ram stuck out for about a metre, while a secondary ram protruded from the prow above the water line, intended to prevent the main ram from smashing too deeply into an enemy hull where it might get stuck. When rammed or otherwise disabled, a trireme would splinter into floating fragments; it would not sink, but neither would it remain afloat to be captured and used by the enemy.

A typical trireme battle would start with lines of opposing ships advancing on one another, like lines of advancing soldiers on land. As the fleets closed, the tactics would kick in: every trierarch (trireme captain) would try to steer between two of the enemy, turning at the right moment to ram one of them broadside. This was the move honed to perfection by Themistokles at the Athenian navy's finest hour at the Battle of Salamis in 480 BC. In the narrow Salamis channel, the unwieldy hulks of the larger Persian fleet proved easy meat for the skilled Greek trireme crews. The result was that a good part of Greece was saved from Asiatic occupation. Greek seamanship was considered the best in the Mediterranean even when Athens and Sparta engaged in their life-or-death struggle known as the Peloponnesian War. Sparta, at first ignorant of naval matters, nevertheless learned quickly, until the Spartan admiral Lysandros smashed the remnants of Athenian sea power at Aigos Potamoi in 404 BC – incidentally, within sight of where the *Averof* was to carry out its first patrols twenty-two centuries later.

As Greece declined in power, giving way to Rome, Greek seamen distinguished themselves as traders and pirates rather than naval personnel. The Byzantine Empire (330–1453) brought Greek dominance back into the eastern Mediterranean. But it was swallowed up by the advancing Muslim Ottoman Turks who employed Greek shipwrights to build and skipper their naval galleys, and Christian Greek slaves to man the oars. The Battle of Lepanto in 1571, where a Christian European fleet demolished the Ottoman galleys under Hayreddin Barbarossa, saw the beginning of the end of Ottoman naval domination in the Mediterranean and its gradual replacement by Spain and the states of Italy. The Greek mainland itself, thanks partly to the contributions of the Koundouriotis family, threw off Turkish rule in the 1820s, and the way was at last open for modern Greece to try to imitate the achievements of Themistokles. The Greeks certainly could boast of a long enough seafaring tradition to nurture such a dream.

Chapter 3

Birth of the *Averof*

For many influential members of the Greek establishment, it was more than just a dream. The Greek revolution of the 1820s had been fuelled by the desire for Greece to join the European family of nations. Once that was done by force of arms, intellectuals yearned to rebuild the classical Greece of old, in territory as well as prestige. This would mean annexing large parts of western Turkey including Constantinople, whose loss in 1453 was (and still is) dramatically mourned in the churches and school books. Not surprisingly, the late nineteenth century saw a powerful movement to take back 'the City', as Constantinople was affectionately known, from the Muslim Turk who had desecrated the Orthodox holy sites, and bring the blessings of Greek civilization back to the downtrodden Greeks of the Ottoman Empire.

Of course, Greece was by no means the only nation to think in such romantic and ambitious terms. Irredentism and expansionism, the sense of a nation's overriding 'natural' destiny, were becoming global phenomena. Statesmen and military officers around the world made sure to read *The Influence of Sea Power on History*, written in 1890 by Alfred Thayer Mahan, an American naval historian. The nub of Mahan's thesis was something which Themistokles would have heartily endorsed – that a country's power depends on trade-borne wealth, which in turn needs to be protected by a powerful navy. The power and prosperity of the British Empire had demonstrated the truth of that. Britain forged ahead in the naval race in 1904 with the development of HMS *Dreadnought*, a sleek and powerful steel battleship that would give its name to a whole class of vessels.

Yet strong rivals to Britain's superiority at sea were arising at the beginning of the twentieth century. Imperial Germany was busy with its own aggressive shipbuilding programme, demonstrated dramatically when Kaiser Wilhelm II sent the warship *Panther* to Agadir in Morocco to thwart French designs in 1911. Instead, it was the sea-sensitive British who were spooked more than the French, and the kaiser had to back down when London beat the war drums. The Americans, too, had just had their imperial moment by trouncing the Spanish in 1898; that war had been triggered by the mysterious destruction of one of America's smartest battleships, the USS *Maine*, in Havana port. On the other side of the world, the Japanese had proved apt pupils of Mahan and by 1905 had defeated the Russians in a quick and ruthless campaign in which the new Japanese pre-dreadnought battleships had played a pivotal part. The lesson of the times was clear: any nation with any pride at all had to have its shiny metal navy.

The turn of the twentieth century was in many ways a paradise for warship designers. Since the first shaky ironclads of the American Civil War era, great strides had been made in strengthening armour while keeping it relatively light, light enough to clothe a ship without affecting its speed. The armour revolution pioneered by the Harvey process was supplemented by Germany's Krupp works, which came up with a special cemented steel twice as strong as ordinary armour and lighter to boot. In Britain, Admiral William White was a keen follower of developments in warship engineering. During a secret visit to Italy in 1896 he became impressed by Italian progress in designing cruisers powerful enough to engage the battleships of stronger powers if need be.

Italy was the pioneer of the armoured cruiser – a battleship in all but name and size, but affordable by smaller powers too poor to pay for conventional battleships. The Italian *Garibaldi* class was a good example; at some 7,500 tons, with just three major guns and protected by 5in of armour, it could make twenty knots and pose a serious threat to a battleship. A number of nations were quick to perceive the advantages of the *Garibaldis*: Argentina bought four and Spain one. Japan snapped up two more originally destined for Argentina, just in time for the Russo-Japanese War where they did sterling work against the Tsar's navy in the Tsushima Strait.

Armoured cruisers, White argued, could 'come to close quarters with the enemy without running undue risks' – a prime requirement for a navy that had relatively few resources yet wished to make its mark in the world's chess game of power. Taking his example from the Italians, White developed his own British armoured cruisers that differed from the continental version in having more vertical armour and larger guns to inflict severer damage on enemy battleships. Yet armour had to be traded for speed; the heavier the vessel, the fewer knots it could attain, and it was some time before a compromise was reached to allow an armoured cruiser to surge to, say, twenty-three knots, as the French navy's *Jeanne d'Arc* reportedly could (and which White seriously doubted). The Entente Cordiale between Britain and France was still some years in the future, and the *Jeanne d'Arc* was the putative main adversary against which White planned his new ships.

Speed was essential, and that in part depended on what boilers were used. French-built Belleville water-tube boilers were just coming on stream, lighter and more efficient than the cylindrical ones used so far. But being new, they suffered from a host of problems, which the Royal Navy tackled aggressively. Just as important was armour. Big new foreign warships were afloat, all of them potentially dangerous to Britain's mastery of the seas: in addition to the *Jeanne d'Arc*, there were Germany's *Fürst Bismarck* (not to be confused with the more famous *Bismarck* of a later era), Russia's hulking big *Rossiya* and the US Navy's new USS *Brooklyn*. The Russian ship was the most thickly armoured, with eight inches of Harvey steel above and below the waterline.

The main fuel in those days was coal, which had an added protection value. Trials had shown that coal packed inside the ship's hull could weaken the impact of a torpedo by absorbing much of the blast. White's idea was to arrange the coal bunkers as protective layers around the vulnerable boilers and engines and along the ship's sides. The idea caught on, and soon the arrangement became standard on Italian-built armoured cruisers.

As the world's secondary navies rushed to furnish themselves with armoured cruisers, Britain's Royal Navy found itself compelled to keep up, even though by about 1905 the type was already sliding into obsolescence. It took the drive and genius of Admiral Sir John Fisher, appointed First Sea Lord the previous year, to come up with a revolution in battleship design with HMS *Dreadnought*. This in turn spurred armoured cruiser builders to come up with new features, such as increases in firing range and the addition of fire-control tops perched on the masts fore and aft. And this was the world of steel and guns in which the *Averof* took form and began its long career.

It was, in fact, something of an accident that this particular armoured cruiser ended up in Greek hands at all. For some years planners in the Greek navy ministry had yearned to acquire a dreadnought, but two factors militated against it. One was the cost of such a vessel – exorbitant for a small country such as Greece – and the other was the opposition of Imperial Germany, which was planning its own *Drang nach Osten*, or drive to the east, for which a strong Greece might prove an obstacle in the Mediterranean.

Moreover, the obvious source of dreadnoughts would be Britain and France, and Kaiser Wilhelm II preferred that the Greeks bought a German-built capital ship which would increase Athens' political dependence on Berlin. Besides, King George I of Greece was a close relative of the kaiser.

The answer was to acquire an armoured cruiser of the successful type being built by the Italians. The keel of what was to become the *Averof* was laid in the Cantiere Navale Fratelli Orlando shipyard at Livorno (Leghorn), Italy, in 1909, based on a 1905 design by Giuseppe Orlando. As the second of a planned series of *Pisa*-class armoured cruisers, it was initially on order for the Brazilian navy, but Brazil had reneged on its payments and work had stopped. Two sister armoured cruisers, what were to become the *Pisa* and *Amalfi* for the Italian navy (Regia Marina), had just been completed in the same yard. Orlando Brothers' reputation was well-established. From its scantlings had emerged four heavy armoured cruisers for the Italians, four more for Argentina, two for Japan and one for Spain. One unfinished ship was left to be claimed, and alarm bells rang in Athens when it became known that the Turkish navy was after it.

Fortunately, there was a government in Athens that had the necessary resolve to obtain the ship. In August 1909 a junta of army and navy officers under Colonel Nikolaos Zorbas had brushed aside the ineffectual civilian government and forced King George to pay more heed to the popular call for 'redeeming' the ethnic Greek populations of the Ottoman Empire. Fortunately, the junta had the foresight to engage the services of the able and energetic Venizelos as prime minister, though without losing the military character that enabled vital decisions to be made with a minimum of political dithering and corruption.

The big problem, of course, was money. Orlando Brothers was prepared to resume work on the incomplete cruiser on behalf of whoever could come up first with a deposit of £250,000 in gold, representing one-quarter of the purchase price. As long as the Ottoman government failed to raise the money, the Greeks had a sporting chance at the ship, and here is where a Greek tycoon came in – though he never knew it, as he had been dead for more than ten years. This was George Averof, a millionaire Greek who had made his fortune in Egypt and had specified in his will that his legacy be used to build a training vessel for the Greek navy. Averof's executors, though, figured that the amount could easily cover the required deposit for Orlando Brothers. That clinched the deal and thus the late George Averof's name was put on the side of the most famous warship in modern Greek history. After a series of modifications to the basic *Pisa*-class design to accommodate Greek requirements, on 12 March 1910 the *Averof*'s hull slid down the slipway at Livorno, its concave prow and formidable ram towering above the cheering and hat-waving crowds.

RHNS *Averof*, despite the great hopes pinned on it, was not the last word in heavy warships of the time, but that didn't matter much. With a length of 140m (459.3ft), a maximum beam of 21m (68.9ft) and a draught of 7.5m (24.6ft), the ship represented a fairly standard example of a pre-dreadnought of the type which the less powerful countries of the world could afford. There were still few enough of the bigger battleships on the world's seas in 1911 to make the armoured cruiser a formidable proposition.

At its launch the *Averof* had a displacement of 9,450 tons, rising to 10,200 tons with a full load, which included a basic complement of 670 officers and enlisted men. It was powered by two vertical four-cylinder triple-expansion reciprocating Italian-made Ansaldo engines, supported by twenty-two French-made Belleville water-tube type boilers. The boilers had to be relatively small because of the requirements of coal firing, hence their large number; they were grouped in four separate boiler rooms to minimize damage from enemy action. The engines delivered a full power of 19,000 shp that could spurt to 21,500 shp in an emergency. The twin screws could push the ship through the water at a top twenty-two and a half knots (though it attained nearly twenty-four knots during its sea trials). Bunker capacity was ordinarily 600 tons of coal, with a maximum capacity of 1,500 tons. Its autonomous range at full speed was 1,400 nautical miles, or 2,600 miles at twelve knots. (So reliable were the triple-expansion Ansaldos that they remain in good working order to this day.)

The *Averof*'s armament was similar to that of its Italian sister ship *Pisa*, but differed in one vital respect – its guns were manufactured by that *par excellence* British supplier of land and naval artillery for the world, Vickers. Almost certainly Basil Zaharoff, by now Vickers' chief foreign salesman, had a hand in the arming of the ship, which bristled with four 28-ton 23.4cm (9.2in) Mark X and eight 14-ton 19.7cm (7.5in) guns partly buried in thick convex turrets on the centreline fore and aft; the former were of 46.6 calibre and the latter 45. The larger guns could hurl a 172kg (380lb) shell with a muzzle velocity of 807m (2,640ft) per second, propelled by a 46.7kg (103lb) explosive charge. The smaller guns carried a 90kg (200lb) shell fired by a 21.3kg (47lb) charge to a muzzle velocity of 792m (2,600ft) per second. Complementing this firepower were sixteen 14lb 7.5cm (2.95in) deck guns (later replaced by anti-aircraft weaponry). Below the waterline were three 53cm (21in) torpedo tubes, one at the stern and two on either side below the bridge (they were later removed after a curious combat mishap).

The turrets and the size of the guns in them were fairly standard for an armoured cruiser of the time; the fore guns could be rotated to fire broadsides in three directions, forward, port and starboard. The turrets were rotated hydraulically on the barbettes, though the guns could be aimed manually in an emergency. Armoured steel sleeves extended from them down to the magazines as protection for the ammunition hoists. One of the more remarkable features of the *Averof* was its fire-control system with optical rangefinders, perched high above the smokestacks so as not to be blinded by the coal smoke.

Apart from its hardware, the *Averof* was as well-protected as any warship could be at the time. The ship's Krupp-type case-hardened steel armour, supplied by Terni of Italy, was applied in a 200mm (7.75in)-thick main vertical belt along the hull sides; the plating tapered to 100mm (3.5in) fore and aft. Armour of a similar thickness protected the upper deck. The main deck was clad in armour of 175mm (6.75in). The gun turrets had 140mm (5.75in) steel, rotating on barbettes 40mm (1.5in) thick. High above, the fire control top had 180mm (7.75in) armour designed to withstand a direct hit from a 23.4cm (9.2in) heavy gun. The *Averof* followed standard Italian design in having its double bottom divided into eighteen watertight compartments from stem to stern.

Hardly was the paint dry on the *Averof*'s hull than the ship sailed into a peculiar political storm. The reason that the RHN was able to acquire such a vessel in the first place, it will be recalled, was that a military-minded revolutionary government had taken power in Athens in 1909. Besides the increased military credits that the regime made available, nationalist sentiment among the public was stoked to fever pitch. The previous year the Cretans had attempted to throw off an international tutelage of great powers and join up with Greece; the attempt had failed, but it had triggered a reaction in the Ottoman Empire: the Young Turk movement (of which more later) which seized power in Constantinople, the capital, and revived the Ottomans' muscular stance in the Balkans.

The new Greek regime had been an outgrowth of unrest in the Greek military that by 1909 had crystallized in an organization known as the Military League. According to its founding statement, the purpose of the Military League was to improve 'the immediate military and naval readiness of the country'. The statement demanded that the war and navy ministries be headed by men approved by the army and navy respectively. Inertia and inefficiency in the previous government triggered the Military League's move on 15 August on a programme of military and economic reform. Among those young naval officers who eagerly seconded the revolt was Sub Lieutenant Alexander Sakellariou whose breast swelled with pride when he was picked to be part of the complement of the *Averof.*

It was a Saturday night, 7 May 1911, when Sakellariou and about 600 other men boarded the steamship *Athenai* for the voyage to the Italian port of La Spezia to pick up the cruiser that was about to complete its sea trials and was ready for commissioning. As the *Athenai* sidled up to the *Averof* at La Spezia a week later, the crew fell silent with awe at the sight of the great ship's smooth lines. The elegance of Italian design was evident in the sophisticated sweep of the hull curvature, subtle superstructure profiling and low turret placement, combining in a shark-like image of cool power. The fire control top tripod behind the foredeck towered over the three vertical smokestacks. But the real objects of admiration were the guns – massive smooth barrels of destruction thrusting out of their streamlined turrets. After lunch on the *Athenai* the crew were able to board the cruiser. Sub Lieutenant Sakellariou was overwhelmed.

An air of enthusiasm overcame me [he would write in his memoirs much later] at the thought that whether I lived or died on this ship, I would enjoy the results of my fight, to secure the liberty of my country! Something told me that this ship's shells would demolish the arrogance of our foes.

The crew mustered on deck in full dress uniform at 10.00 am under a drizzly sky on Monday 16 May for the formal commissioning of the *Averof* under its commander, Captain Ioannis Damianos. The wet weather seemed to have put paid to plans to hoist a silken national flag which a group of wives of the Greek community of Alexandria had sewn for the purpose. But during the morning the weather cleared and the silken flag was duly hoisted. At 5.00 pm the next day the anchor was raised, the throbbing Ansaldos set in motion, and the *Averof* set sail on its first operational mission across the Mediterranean to Algiers for coaling.

On board the cruiser were several British advisers, including a gunnery expert named Salmond who showed the Greek gunners how the shells should be stored in the magazines. After three days in Algiers, fully coaled, Damianos received orders to sail for Spithead on the south coast of England to take part in the Naval Review to mark the coronation of King George V. The Greek royal family was not as closely related to the British as it was to the German, but the royal solidarity was there, and the elderly King George I of Greece naturally wished to show off his country's latest acquisition in naval hardware to Britain, the greatest sea power of the era.

Past Gibraltar the crew of the *Averof* had their first experience of Atlantic swells and fog. As the ship punched and pitched through heavy seas in the Bay of Biscay, Sakellariou marvelled at the stamina of the men in the trawlers which the ship met on its way north. At 11.00 am on 26 May the cruiser bucked the cold winds blowing around the Isle of Wight and put into Southampton at 8.00 pm. The plan for the Naval Review was for Britain's Royal Navy to steam past Spithead in formations of four lines of warships, each line five miles long, with foreign navies making up a fifth line. Sakellariou was the ship's officer sent to get a copy of the review plan; he noted that two ships in front of the *Averof* in the foreign line would be the Ottoman

Turkish armoured cruiser *Hamidiye*, rather smaller than the *Averof* but with a similar three-funnel profile. (He had, of course, no way of knowing that the *Averof* would soon meet the *Hamidiye* in more aggressive conditions.)

'Never before have I seen, and do not expect to see again, such enormous ships ranged before Spithead!' Sakellariou enthused in his diary. The spit and polish and overall organization made a profound impression on him. It was probably the first time Greek naval officers had been brought before the reality of a state-of-the-art pre-First World War navy. Sakellariou sensed that he had been given a glimpse of Britain's Royal Navy at the pinnacle of its historic power, a pinnacle it would never again attain. 'While looking at the British ships I had the wicked thought that perhaps aged Albion had invited us here to show us how puny we were in the face of her immense power.' It was not an unreasonable thought.

As part of the Spithead Naval Review, seamen from the various countries represented were assigned to take part in an athletics contest. Sakellariou was deputed to head the *Averof*'s team. The occasion brought out his full-blown contempt of the Turk, a prejudice shared by almost all Greeks. In his diary he stereotyped his Turkish counterpart from the *Hamidiye* as 'stupid, fat and wearing a fez', and having difficulty understanding the rules of the contest when they were explained to him. Yet Greek-Turkish animosity was mild compared to other ethnic hostilities simmering behind the façade of cooperation at Spithead. The Russian and Japanese crews were the worst, not disguising their hatred of each other – hardly surprising as Japan had soundly walloped the Russians six years before in the Russo-Japanese War. Even more virulent was the British hostility to the Germans. 'What a hatred of the Germans afflicts the British! In all our discussions [the British] never even tried to conceal their enmity.'

The sheer variety of national characters – and prejudices – parading in diverse naval uniforms fascinated Sakellariou. He was particularly struck by the appearance of a Japanese officer; 'young, short, with a shaven head, [making] himself comical by that habit of politeness common to his race.' Sakellariou was at a party one evening, dazzled by the constellation of insignia and medals, when a woman came up to him. 'Are you Greek by any chance?' she asked. She turned out to be from an old Athenian family, married to a British lieutenant commander named Pilchard. She invited him on board her husband's ship – but not before a grumpy and rather inebriated Brazilian officer took him aside to lambaste the British for their supposedly 'false propriety'. (Perhaps, being a Latin, the Brazilian had come on to an Englishwoman and had been rebuffed.)

The Naval Review proper got underway on 9 June, with twenty-one-gun salutes thundering deafeningly from all sides. The day began with the athletics ashore – absent the Turkish team – and ended with a glittering panorama of lighted and flag-bedecked ships stretching like diamonds in the dark water as far as the eye could see. The next day a group of London-based Greek ship owners were ferried to the *Averof,* but if the Greek officers were expecting compliments, they didn't get them. Instead the tycoons (who snobbishly refused to speak in their native tongue) told the officers over a lavish lunch to 'give up dreams of conquest and get to work reorganizing the state'. It wasn't an unreasonable view, but it was arrogantly delivered, and moreover not one which the jingoist Greek officer corps cared to hear at the time. What did rich money-grubbers know about national pride and warfare anyway? The Review ended on 16 June, with the great warships pulling away one by one, the Japanese in particular departing 'in exemplary order'. The *Averof* was scheduled to depart later, so Sakellariou and three other officers took the train to London where they watched King George V riding in state through the city and enjoyed an opera at Covent Garden surrounded by the city's glitterati.[1]

In the evening of 18 June Sakellariou and the others had just returned to Plymouth, where the *Averof* had meanwhile sailed, to find the ship in dry-dock. Approaching Plymouth in thick fog it had run aground when the ram below the waterline encountered a submerged mud bank. The cruiser had lurched some 40yds before coming to a halt, opening several gashes in the hull. It would take about a month to repair the damage, but the damage to the crew's morale was not so easily fixed. The immediate result was that in the morning of 21 June, not six weeks after the *Averof* was commissioned, the crew mutinied.

The enthusiasm and attendant hoopla that had accompanied the commissioning of the armoured cruiser had, in fact, masked a smoking discontent among the crew that the ship's complement of officers wasn't doing its job. There was some basis for the bad feeling. It was the first time the RHN had operated a warship as large and complex as the *Averof,* and the officers, despite initial guidance by a British naval team, still had a lot to learn. The result was that among the enlisted seamen, any irregularity in the ship's functioning, from the unfamiliar English cheddar cheese (as far from *feta* as it was possible to get) to excessive harshness on the part of some officers, was regarded with the darkest suspicions.

Captain Damianos patiently heard out the seamen's list of grievances, delivered by an able seaman as self-appointed crew spokesman, with a degree of sympathy. He was not a strict disciplinarian, and was generally well-liked. But he had to dismiss a wild claim that Lieutenant Commander Dragatsis, in charge of the ammunition stores, had been caught trying to set fire to the cordite to blow the ship up! The officer, according to Sakellariou, had been merely inspecting the empty magazines as the first shipment of shells had not yet arrived from Vickers. He was lighting his way with a candle, as the ship's electric power had a problem, and burning wax had spilled onto some oily rags, igniting a small and easily dousable fire. Potentially more serious was a claim that when the *Averof*'s ram had stuck in the mud off Plymouth, the officers had been partying in the wardroom. The interview ended with the mutineers' demand that Dragatsis and four commanders be dismissed 'or there will be trouble on this ship'.

The episode came as a shock to the well-meaning Captain Damianos, who called a meeting of officers for the following morning. Sakellariou, the youngest officer on board and one of the most zealous, called for severe measures and warned the captain that if he was too lenient he might find himself replaced. The captain's reply stunned all present: 'I wish that would happen!'

Though he was undoubtedly aware that agitators were at work among the mutineers, and not only on his own ship, Damianos was loth to employ force in suppressing the mutiny. Moreover, the malcontents had the sympathy of the great majority of petty officers. Whatever the merits or demerits of the revolt, any use of force against it would come as a severe shock to public opinion in Greece and correspondingly be a cause for joy in arch-foe Ottoman Turkey, which had wanted the ship for itself. It would also undermine cohesion in the RHN which most people believed would soon be called upon to fight a shooting war in the Aegean Sea, and a virtual civil war in the navy was not to be risked. By the evening of 22 June feelings had calmed enough for a regular crew inspection to take place without undue tensions, but the next day a message came through from the navy ministry in Athens that the mutiny be put down by force. Damianos refused to comply. If the ministry insisted, he said, 'I'll take my hat and leave!'

Sakellariou later confronted one of the mutiny ringleaders. 'What do you hope to gain?' he said. 'Look at the mess you're making, compared to the law and order of the British here. We all love our navy – don't you see the danger you're putting it in?'

'Some officers are so bloody harsh!' the seaman replied heatedly. 'They look down their noses at the petty officers and crew. And the language they use to their subordinates is just so inhuman!' Sakellariou was struck dumb; he knew the man had a point.

'We've nothing against you, though, sir,' the seaman added, as if reading Sakellariou's mind, 'even though you're one of the tough ones. But don't think that because you pat us on the back from time to time, we forget it all ...'

The Royal Navy felt at this point that it had to step in. On 27 June Lionel Grant Tufnell, a rear admiral on the RN retired list and former commander of the Royal Naval Barracks at Devonport, addressed the *Averof*'s assembled crew through an interpreter. Tufnell promised that genuine grievances would be redressed and he would submit a report to the Greek navy ministry, but warned the officers at the same time that they would have to modify their autocratic ways and be an inspiration to the enlisted men – in particular, they would have to rid themselves of the pernicious Greek habit of involvement in politics. For an element of political rivalry had accentuated the class warfare which had triggered the mutiny; lower crews tended to be more leftish than the officers, and had no hesitation in showing it, while the officers themselves were split between conservative royalists and adherents of the more radical Military League.

The shells for the magazine arrived by train the following day. Seamen had to carry the heavy ammunition cases, weighing maybe 120lbs or more each, on their backs from the train. Naturally, there was a renewed outburst of mutinous grumbling, so Sakellariou lined them up during an interval.

> I know many of you are tired [he told them]. But our ammunition can't remain here in the open overnight. If anyone feels he can't continue, step forward two paces and I'll excuse him from the duty.

No-one stepped forward. All the shells were in the magazines by nightfall.

Meanwhile, recent editions of the Greek daily press had arrived, bursting with exaggerated and downright fanciful accounts of the mud-bank incident and the mutiny, plus a generous quota of political rabble-rousing. Fortunately for the ruling Military League, and the navy in particular, the brouhaha was not allowed to get out of hand. This was because the able Cretan politician Venizelos held down the posts of prime minister and navy minister. Addressing the Parliament, Venizelos pledged a 'radical housecleaning' of the navy, beginning with the transferral of Captain Damianos, the recall to Athens of four unpopular officers as well as eight of the mutiny ringleaders, and the appointment of Pavlos Koundouriotis as the new skipper of the *Averof*. A feeling of relief settled over the ship.

Repairs to the damaged hull took about six weeks, during which officers were taken on tours of Britain's armour and armaments plants and otherwise kept busy. Meanwhile, Tufnell had been spending constructive time in Greece, reorganizing the RHN and setting a personal example of hard work by staying on bridge duty for up to eighteen hours at a stretch. At 3.00 pm on 10 August, bleary-eyed after partying into the early hours, the crew of the *Averof* took up their stations to prepare for the long-delayed voyage home. It took three more days to take on the required tonnage of coal and supplementary ammunition. Sakellariou watched in some amazement as the seamen worked with a will, with not the slightest sign of the rebellious sentiments of June. The cruiser weighed anchor in Plymouth Sound on 20 August and started home.

Captain Koundouriotis nursed the ship south in favourable weather, testing its speed, which could reach twenty-four knots in smooth seas. Gunnery practice took up much of the leg off the Portuguese coast. When the ship put in at Malta on 29 August, admiring crowds lined the dock. Two days later the last lap of the homeward journey began. The ship was now drawing near to Greek waters and the possibility of a Turkish torpedo attack could not be discounted. But it rounded the southern points of the Peloponnese without incident, to meet the rest of the Greek fleet on 1 September, lined up by Tufnell as a floating guard of honour on the approaches to Piraeus. On the way, Koundouriotis had ordered the helmsman to steer through the Hydra strait in order to pay homage to his native island. The Hydriotes had known he was coming and gathered at the island's tiny port to cheer the great grey hulk as it churned past, while the church bells echoed off the island's crags.

The enthusiasm was greater, of course, on the waterfront of Phaleron, south of Athens, where the *Averof* anchored, surrounded by a milling horde of craft of all sizes. At 4.00 pm Venizelos and Crown Prince Constantine came on board for a formal inspection, and when they left the ship was opened to the ecstatic public.

Everyone, educated or common, employees, fishermen or professionals, as soon as they set foot on the deck made the sign of the cross [Sakellariou wrote]. Some knelt to kiss the deck, and all had the expression of someone freed from a great mental burden … it was the great warship of the people.

Chapter 4

Young Turks, Old Ships

At the start of the twentieth century the Ottoman Empire was about 500 years old and drawing slowly yet inexorably towards its close. Over the past hundred or so years nationalist revolts had deprived it of key European territories such as Greece and the Balkans; elsewhere, such as in Egypt and Palestine, its administrators and garrisons were under threat from the newly-awakened and restive Arab peoples. By the 1880s Britain had taken over Egypt as a key way-station on the all-important imperial route to India, further cramping the Turkish sultan's domains. Russia to the north coveted the Bosporus and Constantinople itself as an outlet to the warm Mediterranean. From all four directions of the compass the sultan was on the defensive. Despite several bold military and political reforms in the late nineteenth century, the Ottoman Empire was riddled by paralysing corruption and a feeling of fatalistic helplessness in the face of the new aggressive world powers of Britain, France and Germany.

From the Ottoman Turks' conquest of Constantinople in 1453 and the erasure of the Greek Byzantine Empire to about the middle of the nineteenth century Ottoman Turkish sea power in the Mediterranean had experienced a startling rise and a slow but irreversible decline, to the point that it needed just a push from a second-rate European power to all but sink it. In the fifteenth and sixteenth centuries the Ottomans' main maritime rival was Venice. Venetian control of Mediterranean trade was the threat and stimulus that moved the Sublime Porte (as the sultan's palace in Constantinople was known) to build up a formidable Ottoman navy, manned in part by seafarers from subjugated Greece. A large naval base was set up at Gallipoli. The commercial rivalry was accentuated by a yet more profound religious one: the Ottomans were nothing if not staunch Muslims, inheriting the anti-Western animus of another Turk, Saladin of Crusades fame, and ideologically committed to fighting Western power wherever it was found.

By 1498 Sultan Bayezid II had set in motion a crash shipbuilding programme that struck alarm into the Venetians and Spaniards. The new Ottoman navy proved its worth the following year when Bayezid's galleys overran Venetian possessions in Greece. The biggest tactical success was the seizure of the Venetian fort at Lepanto (modern Navpaktos) on the Gulf of Corinth, a move that was to have momentous consequences seven decades later. The Ottomans also seized the strategic Greek peninsular port of Preveza (the scene of the pivotal Battle of Actium in 31 BC where Octavian vanquished Mark Antony). Bayezid's grandson Süleyman I (known as the Magnificent) kept up the pressure on the West, sending his armies deep into central Europe as far as the outskirts of Vienna.

On the naval side Süleyman was fortunate in securing talented men for his maritime commands. One was Piri Reis, an able admiral and cartographer who lost his life trying to eject the Portuguese from the Strait of Hormuz. Yet abler was a renegade Greek known by his mixed Muslim-Italian name of Hayreddin Barbarossa. Already the sultan had formally claimed to be the *padisha* (emperor) of 'the White and Black Seas', the 'White Sea' being what the Ottomans called the Mediterranean. Barbarossa (whose name means Redbeard) helped bring that sweeping claim close to reality.

Barbarossa was at the height of his powers when in 1538 he went up against the renowned Italian admiral Andrea Doria, the chief naval commander of Holy Roman Emperor Charles V. The main theatres of the conflict were the waters around Greece and the Ionian and Adriatic seas. Both the Christian and Muslim realms needed this corner of southeast Europe to secure their trade routes; the eastern Mediterranean was a maritime crossroads, a many-stranded vital web where merchantmen of many nations, from England to Arabia, needed to ply to maintain their countries' commercial prosperity. Even though America had just been 'discovered', the New World was yet to be exploited in any big way; most of Europe still viewed the Levant as the continent's main source of trade. Besides, sitting squarely at the eastern end of the Mediterranean was the venerated Holy Land; the Christian nations' desire to keep it open for pilgrimage matched the Muslims' desire to keep it for themselves.

Doria, under Venetian prodding, sailed an imperial-papal fleet to Preveza to try and pry Barbarossa, now styled *kapudan-i derya*, or grand admiral of the fleet, from that stronghold. On viewing the fort, Doria had second thoughts – or perhaps, as his enemies claimed, he made a secret deal with the Ottoman admiral. Whatever the truth, Doria withdrew without attacking, and Barbarossa damaged several imperial vessels in the pursuit. That victory encouraged Barbarossa to range aggressively farther afield. Helping him was France, which saw in the Ottoman Empire a handy counterweight against the Holy Roman Empire and the papacy. Fleets of Ottoman galleys swept across the western Mediterranean in 1543–44, and at one point Florence had a serious scare when Turkish forces made a landing on the Italian coast.

The naval threat to the West came to a head in 1571. Sultan Selim I (named Yavuz, or the Grim, for his scowling features and brusque manner) had just expanded his Mediterranean holdings by capturing Cyprus. The prestige of the Ottoman sultanate was at its giddiest height – the list of Selim's formal titles ran to no fewer than seventy-four words, ending neatly (almost as afterthoughts) with 'Destroyer of the Christian Faith and Dominator of the Universe'. He had reason to puff himself up. His galleys were making life difficult for Venetian colonies along the Adriatic coast and he no doubt hoped that soon Venice itself would fall to the red crescent. But this time the West was serious about stopping him. On 7 October a Christian fleet under the 24-year-old Don John of Austria, a half-brother of Philip II of Spain (whose own Armada was destined to come to grief in the English Channel seventeen years later), dropped anchor in the calm blue waters of the Gulf of Patras, just west of the Rhion narrows. Don John was in command of 210 Venetian, Florentine, Neapolitan, Genoese and Spanish galleys and galleasses aiming to force the narrows and capture the Ottoman fort at Lepanto. Opposing him were some 260 Ottoman vessels under Barbarossa's successor as grand admiral, Müezzinzade Ali Pasha. In the ensuing encounter, known to history as the Battle of Lepanto, Don John's imperial fleet trounced the Ottomans through superior seamanship and artillery fire. The Ottoman Turkish navy never completely recovered from the blow.

It wasn't until the early eighteenth century that the Ottomans looked to despised Europe for advice in military reforms, and to France in particular. The Constantinople admiralty was reorganized and ship construction steered in the direction of three-deck galleons which finally saw off the old galleys. French officers, some of them converts to Islam, improved training methods. Sultan Selim III accelerated the process, authorizing subjects such as gunnery and navigation to be added to the naval curriculum. As a result, for the first time the Ottoman Empire could boast a small but capable corps of naval officers familiar with Western thinking. In the early nineteenth century Selim's successor Mahmud II put the military modernization drive into high gear, eliminating the mediaeval crack but politically unreliable Jannisary (*Yeni Cheri*, or New Forces) corps, and laying the foundations for a new national army. It is said that Mahmud himself was dramatically converted to the merits of steam over sail when a frigate he was on almost capsized in a strong gale and was saved by being towed to shore by two foreign steamships.

The navy, meanwhile, had suffered another devastating blow at the hands of the British, French and Russians at the Battle of Navarino in 1827, during the Greek War of Independence. In later years American experts were called in to help rebuild the fleet in the main arsenal at the Halic naval station in the Golden Horn. But before the process could be completed, the new Ottoman fleet was caught napping and all but pounded to matchwood by Russian Admiral Pavel Nakhimov at Sinop on the Black Sea in November 1853. One vessel that escaped was the hulking, 128-gun *Mahmudiye*, little different from a ship of the Napoleonic Wars even if it was the biggest warship in the world at that time. In its thirty-two year career the *Mahmudiye* saw action only once, at Sevastopol later in the Crimean War. Even though Turkish gunners were scorned as far from competent, Nakhimov was killed in the action.

At that time the Ottoman navy's ships were, according to one source, 'mere baubles for the sultan … expected perhaps to appear offshore to intimidate a foe, but hardly ever to fight'. But by the 1880s the Turks had acquired a good number of expensive ironclads, though in the process Sultan Abdülhamid II (1877–1909) almost bankrupted his country. Pervasive corruption also played its part. Time after time, funds destined to build up and modernize the navy were diverted into private pockets, often with the sultan's blessing. Abdülhamid was not only corrupt but also paranoid. Besides appearing not to have the slightest interest in the sea or naval affairs, he harboured such a suspicion of his senior admirals – constantly fearing a mutiny – that he kept the ironclads permanently anchored at Halic within view of his palace for nineteen years. As for the officer corps, 'too often their knowledge of navigation was limited to making coins travel directly into their own pockets'.

A modern navy could hardly flourish under such blatant graft and abuse. The only redeeming factor was the body of foreign technical advisers who ran the local shipyards, assembling warships from imported British parts and weapons. British business interests meanwhile had done a good job of bribing the sultan's court to acquire the Ottoman Empire's coal deposits and thus control the source of the navy's fuel. But it wasn't enough to avert a second Turkish defeat at Russian hands in January 1878, when Admiral Stepan Makarov sank the 163-ton gunboat *Intibah* by the first known successful use of Whitehead torpedoes. Abdülhamid responded by ordering forty torpedo boats over the next twenty years, plus a couple of Nordenfelt submarines more for prestige than anything else – because the Greeks already had one – but few Turkish seamen proved willing to risk their necks in what were justifiably feared as death-traps.

A further debacle occurred in a brief war with Greece in 1897. The Ottoman Empire lost Crete because the bulk of the navy, rotting at its moorings in the Golden Horn for two decades, was in no position to ferry troops to the island in any appreciable quantity. That finally knocked some sense into the sultan. His government quickly approved the purchase of two 10,000-ton battleships and four armoured cruisers, but the treasury, burdened with huge pre-existing debts to British and German shipbuilders, was hardly in a position to pay for them. It took months of negotiations on discounts for the government to afford three armoured cruisers, eight destroyers and several smaller gunboats. One of the cruisers, the *Drama*, never reached Constantinople; it was sequestered by the Italian government while still on the scantlings at the Ansaldo yard in Genoa – a victim of the sultan's debts to Italian weapons manufacturers. Yet by 1907 there was enough of a solid basis for a new navy for a British naval mission to travel to Turkey to organize the training.

Abdülhamid probably didn't know it, but his days were numbered. For more than twenty years many Turkish army and naval officers, educated in western ways, had been chafing at the corruption and degeneration rampant in the sultan's administration. The officer corps was thus a fertile recruiting ground for the Young Turks, an organization that combined a desire for western-style reforms with a strong streak of nationalist pride. In the Turkish military this movement took the form of the Committee for Union and Progress, which agitated for radical reforms at high level. These officers were highly alarmed at the constant chipping away at the Empire by rebellious subject peoples in the Balkans and the West's support for them. The sense of national humiliation was intense.

The Ottoman army's Third Corps based in Macedonia – geographically closest to the sources of modernizing European influence – was the first to translate the agitation into action. Abdülhamid sent staff officers to investigate the unrest and in particular apprehend one young officer named Enver Bey, who fled before he could be seized. This attempt at repression only inflamed feelings further and soon the Second Corps, based at Edirne, joined what was developing into a full-scale military mutiny. The Third Corps mutineers proclaimed a national constitution in the Macedonian town of Monastir, forcing the sultan to endorse the decision and extend it to the realm as a whole, while appointing senior officials amenable to the CUP.

Those days of July 1908 were heady ones for the Ottoman Empire. To many liberals and intellectuals the army had dragged the sultanate, figuratively kicking and screaming, into the modern era. But eastern European powers, far from supporting the change, used this moment of Ottoman weakness to seize territory. Crete joined itself to Greece, Austria–Hungary gobbled up Bosnia and Herzegovina and Bulgaria proclaimed its outright independence. To complicate matters, in April 1909 the largely Albanian-manned First Corps in Constantinople occupied the centre of the city demanding a militantly Islamic administration and adoption of *sharia* law. Enver, by now the military attaché in Berlin and a *pasha* (general), rushed back with his chief of staff, a clever and highly capable young officer named Mustafa Kemal, to join General Mahmud Shevket in Salonika in forming a 30,000-strong so-called Action Army (*Hareket Ordusu*) that marched on Constantinople and dispersed the Muslim reactionaries on 24 April.

Shevket and Enver acted quickly, formally deposing Abdülhamid and packing him off into exile, replacing him with his pliable brother who took the throne as Mehmet V. This man was a mere puppet of the CUP and the Young Turks, who now held *de facto* power throughout the empire. Special anti-insurgency squads were formed in the army to deal with Balkan guerrillas. Shevket himself expanded his powers to those of a military dictator on the Cromwellian model. But faced with growing opposition to an authoritarian rule little different from that under Abdülhamid, Shevket was pressured into allowing limited freedoms, though always at the sufferance of the CUP. Then in October 1912 Greece, Bulgaria, Serbia and Montenegro, sensing the imminent demise of the Ottoman system, declared war on the empire.

Turkey's new military masters may have had problems in enforcing their new system, and may have gone about it thuggishly at times, but one thing they made sure of was to build up the navy as well as the army. Barely two months after the Action Army marched on Constantinople, Admiral Sir Douglas Gamble arrived from Britain to supervise the programme of naval construction and modernization.

From the first, Gamble had to put up with insistent and outrageous demands for bribes from government officials; his stern resistance to this venality eventually got him sent back to Britain, but not before he earned the respect of Turkish naval officers by conducting the navy's first real seagoing manoeuvres in twenty years in the Sea of Marmara. This respect, in defiance of official Ottoman policy, was to last through the First World War.

In August 1910 the navy received two second-hand German battleships clad in Krupp nickel-steel armour. They were probably all that could be afforded since, as we have seen, the Greek government and its late benefactor's largesse had beaten the Turks to the ship under construction at the Orlando yard that would become the *Averof.* Over the next two years the Turks stabilized their battle fleet at twenty-six ships of the line to confront the Greek fleet which had by now become the most serious threat to Ottoman power in the Aegean.

By late 1912 the Turkish navy had been organized – thanks largely to Admiral Gamble's underappreciated efforts – into the Bosporus, Dardanelles and Black Sea fleets. The flagship of the Bosporus fleet (and largest ship in the navy) was the armoured cruiser *Barbaros Hayreddin,* a German-built pre-dreadnought (formerly the *Kürfürst Friedrich Wilhelm*) commanded by Captain Enver Hakki, accompanied by the *Turgut Reis* (ex-*Weissenburg*), commanded by Captain Ismail Ahmer, and twelve smaller ships. The Dardanelles fleet guarded the entrance to the Sea of Marmara and was made up of the cruiser *Mesudiye,* commanded by Captain Tevfik Bey, who was also the fleet commander. Heading the Black Sea fleet was Captain Hüseyin Rauf, whose flagship was the cruiser *Hamidiye,* accompanied by the *Mecidiye.* Captain Rauf in *Hamidiye* spent most of 1912 raiding Greek merchant ships and shore installations with some success. But that was the Ottoman navy's last hurrah, as by December nemesis had arrived in the form of RHNS *Averof.*

Chapter 5

The Ship that Won a War

In the first decade of the twentieth century it was clear to the world that the Ottoman Empire was at the exit door of history. But some European powers didn't want to see it completely ejected. One of them was Britain. For some time Britain had been trying to keep it intact as a valuable staging-post on the all-important imperial connection with India. But by 1909 even Britain was reading the writing on the wall. There was no way the increasingly despotic Sultan Abdülhamid II could be defended against a wave of hostile media-fuelled western liberal opinion, while the Turks' lack of administrative and military progress earned the contempt of chancelleries all over Europe. This contempt was strongest in the Orthodox Christian nations of Russia and those eastern European areas such as Greece, Bulgaria and Serbia, which had been under Ottoman rule for centuries. Resurgent nationalism in these areas backed by an assertive Orthodox clergy chafed at the bit to deal the death blow to the Muslim sultan's power once and for all.

Greece had the most ambitious aims. The country had been reborn in 1829 after throwing off Ottoman rule in a fierce eight-year rebellion with the help of Britain, France and Russia. In 1909 independent Greece was limited to the Peloponnese in the south, and a wide strip of territory running along the northern shore of the Gulf of Corinth including Athens, and the plain of Thessaly. Still under the sultan's rule were extensive ethnically-Greek lands in Epiros and Macedonia. These, the military-backed government in Athens decided, had to be brought into the Greek fold. Romantic visionaries eyed Constantinople itself, the Greeks' thousand-year Cathedral City, the heart of the gilded glories of the Byzantine Empire, imagined to be waiting to be freed from the alien infidel's chains. At least, that's what the Orthodox clergy, the schools and the press unceasingly dinned into people's minds. One stroke with the mailed fist, and the Cathedral City would be back in the Greek bosom, where she belonged.

The *Averof* at last was that mailed fist, and on its very deck Venizelos proclaimed the national crusade: 'Greece will not remain small. She will become great.' The ship had become a simultaneous symbol and microcosm of the whole Greek nation.

This was partly thanks to the untiring efforts of Admiral Tufnell, who toughened up the Greek navy crews with constant manoeuvres in all weathers. It was while the *Averof* was anchored off Volos during one such exercise that news came of the outbreak of war between the Ottoman Empire and Italy, which had seized the chance to tear off some of the sultan's outlying domains in North Africa. The manoeuvres continued, Tufnell giving the crews no rest, for a whole year. During that time the light cruisers *Hydra*, *Spetsai* and *Psara* switched to smokeless gunpowder, enhancing their firepower. Two new destroyers, the *Nea Genea* and *Keravnos*, were acquired, while in July 1912 an order was placed for a 13,000-ton armoured cruiser in Germany's Bremer Vulkan shipyard, to be sheathed in new American Bethlehem steel.

Sabre-rattling was loud on both sides of the Aegean. The Greek army conducted manoeuvres north of Athens; Athenians looked up into their blue sky one day to see the country's first military aeroplane sputtering past the Acropolis, piloted by Captain Dimitrios Kamberos, a national aviation pioneer. In the navy

Lieutenant Sakellariou worked on a gunnery manual for the *Averof*'s gun crews and had the satisfaction of having it endorsed, printed and distributed by the navy ministry. The Italian navy had not been inactive; it was now shelling the Kumkale fort at the entrance to the Dardanelles and taking steps to occupy the Dodecanese islands to the south. The Greeks wanted a chunk of the action before it was too late. On 19 August Sakellariou had just boarded the *Hydra*, to which he had been transferred, when he was accosted by fellow-officers. 'There's going to be war,' they said, 'and soon.' Around him were the signs of urgency: round-the-clock repair shifts, ammunition packaging and men scurrying back and forth. A week later he found the same frantic atmosphere in the navy ministry, with telegraphs clacking ceaselessly and men running about with requisition and purchase orders. Then on 10 September, as if on cue, the Athens press began a cannonade of bellicose articles. In response, the Ottomans mustered 70,000 men around Edirne – athwart the main route to Constantinople – for manoeuvres.

Venizelos had a personal stake in a scrap with the Ottoman Empire. He hailed from Crete, and was naturally eager to see his native island, once in the sultan's domains, firmly in Greek hands. The only way it could be assured was through force of arms. Thus when Bulgaria, Serbia and Montenegro combined to raise some 550,000 troops and place them on a war footing, Greece eagerly joined in, pledging 120,000 men and its fleet. Greece's military-backed government had meanwhile overhauled its military establishment, setting up a Joint Army and Navy Staff to coordinate inter-service operations. The discredited politicians were elbowed out of military decision-making.

The RHN, for its part, had greatly benefited from a fund set up in 1900 to channel bequests and port revenues into the purchase of new warships. Within six years the fund had bankrolled the acquisition of eight destroyers: the *Sphendoni, Nike, Doxa, Thyella, Navkratousa, Velos, Aspis* and *Lonchi*. Part of the fund also supplemented the late George Averof's bequest to acquire the jewel in the crown, the *Averof*. More new ships arrived in late summer 1912: the large destroyers *Leon, Panthir, Aetos* and *Ierax* from Britain's Cammell Laird shipyard, and the aforementioned *Keravnos* and *Nea Genea* from Germany. The submarine *Delfin* sailed into the fleet's lineup on 5 October, newly-built in Toulon, France. This brought the fleet strength of the RHN to thirty-three ships of the line: four armoured cruisers, fourteen destroyers, one submarine, six torpedo boats, six gunboats, one troop transport and one minelayer.

Advances were being made in naval tactical thinking. By 1911 the advantages of the fast and manoeuvrable armoured cruiser were being taught to cadets in the Piraeus naval academy. One instructor, Commander Pelopidas Tsoukalas, told aspiring naval officers how such a ship ought to be handled:

> An armoured cruiser should get itself swiftly within range of the enemy. It may sound paradoxical, but that's the only way to exploit the superior firepower ... The intensity of fire is itself good protection.

Simply put, an armoured cruiser taking on a battleship in a one-to-one fight would quickly find itself outgunned. On the contrary, steaming boldly into harm's way behind a curtain of relentless fire would momentarily deprive the enemy battleship of the advantage. Such audacity, it was theorized, would put the enemy gunners off their aim, and by the time they collected themselves the attacker's first salvoes would have done their damage. Taking pages from famous naval commanders from Themistokles to Lord Nelson, Tsoukalas injected a tough Spartan element into his lectures: 'A good naval commander has always shown his worth at close quarters. If you want to win, you have to take risks!'[1] Captain Koundouriotis, the naval academy commandant at the time, duly took note.

The Balkan allies' initial strategy was to attack Ottoman forces simultaneously from several directions and throw them on the defensive, uniting in a drive on Constantinople. Defending the European part of Turkey and the capital were 346,000 Turkish troops in seven army corps that initially had orders to stand firm. But on the eve of hostilities the orders were scrapped in favour of attacks on the Bulgarian and Greek fronts. On 4 October 1912 Crown Prince Constantine, the commander-in-chief of the Greek army, ordered the units in Thessaly to strike north into Ottoman-held Macedonia. The Turks put up a strong resistance at Elassona on 6 October and Deskati two days later, before retiring. A more decisive battle at the Sarandaporos River on 9–10 October saw the encircled Turkish forces suffer their first major defeat in the Balkan Wars. On the Greeks pushed, with the aim of seizing the prized port city of Salonika, which was also the goal of the Bulgarians and Serbs. The Greeks got there first and officially annexed it on 26 October, giving it its present name of Thessaloniki to great national rejoicing. The first major Greek objective had been met, at a cost of some 300 soldiers killed and a couple of thousand wounded.

Before moving on Constantinople, however, the Greeks had to see to unfinished business in the north. The regions now occupied by Macedonia and Albania were full of ethnic Greek communities that had been agitating to be free of Ottoman rule and to be included in a greater Greek homeland. The influential popular press rang with calls for their 'liberation' and no government in Athens could afford not to heed them. The army in Thessaly pressed north into what later became Albania, occupying Korcë and its environs. There the

Greeks halted, as they were now almost at the border of Serbia. In January 1913 it was the turn of the western Greek army to punch northwards into Epiros from Arta, under Prince Constantine, who had transferred himself there from the northern front. Fighting mud and snow, the Greeks ejected the Turks from the key town of Ioannina on 22 February, causing more celebrations in Athens. But by then the RHNS *Averof* had already won its first laurels.

Rear-Admiral Koundouriotis' first show of force took place off Mudros Bay on the Turkish-held island of Limnos, when on 6 October 1912 the *Averof* turned its guns on the main port and sent a launch to demand the surrender of the island to the Greeks 'within the hour'. The Turkish garrison refused, so Koundouriotis sent the destroyer *Doxa* to collect a battalion of marines to occupy Limnos. While the *Doxa* was away, four more destroyers patrolled the sea between Limnos and the Dardanelles strait, stopping and inspecting all merchant shipping going through it. The marine battalion, plus two field guns, turned up the following day, its commanding officer climbing onto the rain-drenched deck of the *Averof* to receive his orders to occupy Limnos, which the Turkish garrison abandoned with only token resistance, leaving thirty-five prisoners.

At this, the *Averof*'s first real victory, morale among the crew skyrocketed. Every man on board knew that a scrap with the Turkish navy was imminent. Sakellariou came upon a seaman who was busy polishing the shells in the magazine. When asked why he was taking the trouble over that rather purposeless task, the seaman replied: 'What will those Turcos think of us if we send them grubby shells, sir?' Other crewmembers chalked on the shells the names of the intended targets: *Barbaros, Turgut Reis, Mesudiye.* The men were also cheered by news of the army's successes on the Macedonian front. A throng of coalers and other supply ships flanked the *Averof* in Mudros Bay, adding to the bustle and general air of optimism.

Koundouriotis was as impatient as anyone. 'Why isn't the [enemy] showing himself?' Sub Lieutenant Katsouros reports the rear-admiral as exclaiming, 'I've been waiting for him for three days.' Katsouros' diary entry of 11 October is typical of the perfervid mood of the time:

> We continue to patrol, carrying out inspections, challenging the Turkish fleet with sirens and searchlights. But it knows what's awaiting it, and to our huge disappointment continues to hide, retreating even deeper into its lair. Morale among the crews is excellent, and everyone yearns to hear the guns of the *Averof* in battle, when we will either shatter the Turkish fleet or find a glorious tomb in the watery embrace of the sea.

Again, the following day:

> The radio telegraph from Athens [reports that] the Turks ... slaughtered seventy women and children and a priest ... We are horrified at this grim news of the barbarians, and our hatred is increased against these despicable foes of Christianity who, while slaughtering the weak, avoid like cowards a showdown with the Fleet ... A large British steamship laden with coal for the Turkish government has been captured by the destroyer *Velos* off Tenedos. The cargo was confiscated as war booty and used to fuel our Fleet. God is protecting us.

More ship inspections followed, and where they were found to be carrying arms, such as in the British–flagged SS *Woolwich*, the ships were arrested and the cargoes confiscated. One particular prize catch was a group of Turkish officers and the Vali (governor) of Smyrna, who were taken on board the *Averof* as prisoners.

The next Aegean island to submit under the threat of the cruiser's guns was Imvros, which surrendered peacefully on 18 October as the ethnic Greek population wept with joy. On the following day it was the turn of Samothraki, its Turkish garrison fleeing into the hills. Commander Nikolaos Votsis, in command of Torpedo Boat 11, sank the Ottoman cruiser *Feth-i Bülend* anchored in Thessaloniki harbour, earning a cable of congratulations from the navy minister. As the autumn progressed, the weather in the Aegean gradually worsened and rough seas often hindered destroyer patrols. Yet the island of Tenedos fell, again without a struggle, on 24 October. The island had been strategically important as far back as the Trojan War, when it served as a naval and supply base for the Greeks in their years-long struggle to neutralize Troy. Lying just ten miles from the entrance to the Dardanelles, Tenedos was now seen, in Katsouros' words, as 'the cork that would bottle up the Turkish fleet'. Koundouriotis sent an aggressive signal to the Turkish fleet commander: 'Have occupied Tenedos. Am waiting for you.' Well might the chaplain of the *Averof* call on the Almighty during the service on Sunday 28 October to 'bless us, your worshippers, so that the enemy fleet can come out'.

The ensuing weeks saw more bloodless victories. The Greek flag was hoisted on Mount Athos on 3 November. Remarkable scenes unfolded on the waterfront of Mytilini, the chief port of Lesvos, where young girls and old men wept; some rowed up in boats to kiss the steel plates of the *Averof*'s hull. Sakellariou personally delivered the call for surrender to the Turkish governor, who wanted twenty-four hours to consider Koundouriotis' call to give up the fort of Mytilini, but the Greek admiral would give him just ninety minutes (he had already had eight Turkish prisoners shot for alleged 'crimes' and was in no mood for dickering). When that deadline passed a regiment of Greek troops began landing on Lesvos, sending the

2,000 or so Ottoman defenders fleeing to the hills. When the Greek flag rose over the fort, the thunder of the *Averof*'s twenty-one-gun salute blotted out the band playing the national anthem. An American correspondent for the *New York Herald* came on board with reports of fear and apprehension in the Turkish quarter of Mytilini, followed by the local foreign consuls. Captain Damianos, the former skipper of the *Averof*, sailed up that afternoon with the destroyers *Esperia, Makedonia, Keravnos* and *Nea Genea*.

Rough seas on 9 November kept the cruiser anchored at Mudros, though the destroyers had to keep going out; the *Aspis* narrowly avoided disaster in the towering waves. News arrived that Torpedo Boat 14 had sunk a Turkish gunboat off Aivali. At night, sea birds attracted and dazzled by the ship's searchlights would fly into them, providing the crews with an unexpected food bonus. That was the time that Sakellariou became acquainted with officers of Greece's ally Bulgaria and instantly disliked them – 'primitive and bestial, with whom we could never get along'. There were reports that in West Macedonia and Thrace the Bulgarians were burning everything in their path, discrediting the cause of the Balkan allies and giving a propaganda advantage to the Ottomans.

As the northern Aegean islands were falling to the RHN and its marines like ripe fruit, the Ottoman imperial navy found it lacked the reflexes to react quickly. The only serious action came from Captain Hüseyin Rauf, the commander of the *Hamidiye*, who became a serious nuisance to Greek merchant shipping in the Black Sea and bombarded Balkan shore installations with some success. Some of these bombardments, especially of Bulgarian troop formations, were hopelessly botched, killing more civilians than soldiers. But with the *Averof* and its sister ships ranging freely over what had until now been an Ottoman sea, fast action was needed in the Aegean. Rauf's hit-and-run tactics were not enough. The new Greek fleet had to be stopped before it could butt through the Dardanelles and steam up to Constantinople itself. Captain Ramiz Bey, the Turkish fleet commander, on 25 November was ordered to Canakkale where his fleet was spotted by Greek sea patrols. Ramiz's plan was to draw Koundouriotis' fleet closer towards the entrance to the Dardanelles where the big shore batteries at Cape Helles and Kumkale – practically where the Greek fleet had been beached during the Trojan War – could be brought to bear on the Greeks.

But as any student of naval history could have told Ramiz Bey, the Greeks had seen it all before. It was just a few miles up the Dardanelles strait that the Athenian fleet had been caught by surprise and shattered by the Spartans and their allies in 404 BC, largely because the Athenian commander had been careless and had been caught with his fleet in narrow waters. No Greek naval commander worth his salt would risk that again, even if it was two and a half millennia ago. Koudouriotis, therefore, kept his ships well away from the entrance to the strait, hoping to lure Ramiz into the open sea where the *Averof* could manoeuvre freely.

Neither commander got what he wanted. Ramiz Bey was unwilling to risk an open-sea engagement, so on 1 December 1912, with the weather slightly improved, he sent the armoured cruiser *Mecidiye* on a cautious reconnaissance. Four Greek destroyers sailed aggressively to meet it and there was a brief exchange of fire before the *Mecidiye* scurried back to the safety of the strait. In mid-November the *Averof* had sailed north to the port of Dedeagach (present-day Alexandroupolis) to threaten the Turkish fort there, while farther east other units of the RHN had taken the island of Chios, with some casualties. Now with the reported appearance of the *Mecidiye*, the *Averof* hastened through the rough waters to the patch of sea between Imbros and Tenedos, directly in the path of any vessel emerging from the Dardanelles and entering the Aegean Sea.

In this age of near-smokeless and nuclear fuels, it's difficult to imagine the sheer intimidating impression made by a coal-burning warship. At full speed, thick impenetrable black smoke would belch from its smokestacks as its concave prow thrust menacingly through the waves. The black smoke itself was a symbol of power equal to that of the smoke from the guns. But even then, there were differences in the kind of smoke emitted by various grades of coal. Early on 3 December, with the *Averof* and eight other warships waiting like cats outside a mouse hole, Koundouriotis turned his binoculars on the hills of the Gallipoli peninsula and saw smoke rising from behind them. It could mean only one thing: Ramiz was finally coming out to do battle. The Turkish commander probably didn't realize that his cruisers' fuel – low-grade anthracite from the Zonguldak mines – produced a smoke that was 'dirtier' and hence more visible at large distances than the coal used by the Greek fleet. Ramiz's dirty coal betrayed him. Thus it was that when he emerged from the strait, Koundouriotis was ready.

A gentle north-easterly breeze ruffled the water, which was much calmer than it had been in many days. A brilliant sun was climbing out of the Anatolian shore and the tail end of the Gallipoli peninsula stood out clearly in the crystalline air. Sakellariou was just coming off a four-hour stint as officer of the watch at 8.00 am when the first Turkish ships nosed into view – five destroyers led by the cruiser *Mecidiye* steaming south hugging the mainland coast off Troy. Sakellariou raced to the open bridge to tell the admiral. 'Thank God!' Koundouriotis breathed, making the sign of the cross. Katsouros the engineer officer noted that Koundouriotis' words were, 'Let 'em come now,' and that he pinned a small gold cross to the left side of his tunic. Within minutes the Turkish heavies appeared: first Ramiz's flagship, the *Barbaros Hayreddin*, followed by the *Turgut Reis*, coastal defence cruiser *Mesudiye* and *Asar-i Tewfik*.

The *Averof*'s crew had been in a heady state of optimism for days. A rumour had sped through the ship that the image of Saint Nicholas, the Orthodox patron saint of mariners, had been seen on a powder bucket; when Sakellariou went to investigate, he claimed he could clearly make out the saint's 'white beard and halo'. Mock funeral services were held below decks for the imminent demise of the Turkish ships. Reality supervened when the bugle sounded for battle stations; it took the crew some time to realize that this at last was the real thing and not another drill. The cruiser's decks were the scene of near-chaos, with medics and fire-fighters running about shouting instructions; above their heads the great Vickers gun barrels swung about to fire their first shots in anger. The sick bay was cleared to make room for the expected casualties; bulkheads were hurriedly sealed. A signal went out to the destroyer *Velos* to race to Tenedos and notify the rest of the destroyer force to join the cruisers with all speed; the *Delfin* was ordered to dive and attack the Turks at will. 'The enemy is very close at hand and shortly there will be a battle,' Koundouriotis radioed to the navy ministry before carrying out a hasty inspection of the gun positions and encouraging the crews.

The Turkish commander, of course, knew very well where the Greek ships were; his tactical plan was probably to hit them before they could get any nearer the straits. At about 9.00 am Ramiz in the *Barbaros Hayreddin* veered sharply northwest to get into position, leading the three cruisers. When the Turks were spotted, Koundouriotis' fleet had been on a south-western heading; he at once ordered his ships to about-face and steam northeast on a convergence course with Ramiz. Koundouriotis remained on the *Averof*'s open bridge directing the action; he ordered his destroyer escort to move parallel to the cruisers two miles to the west. At 9.10 am, when the flagships were rather less than thirteen miles apart, the Turks opened fire. Sakellariou, in command of the fore starboard gun turret, saw the gun flashes and stiffened, relaxing only when the shells fell short. Nonetheless, the ship's decks were drenched in spray from the columns of water. A second Turkish salvo also missed.

On board the cruiser *Hydra* Dionysios Lourentzos, a reserve gunnery officer, noticed that the usual banter and joking among the crew was missing, and many faces were pale. The first Turkish salvo fell into the sea 50 yards away. More enemy shells screamed overhead 'as thick as hail,' raising sea plumes 'like huge white cypress trees'. The *Hydra* was about to return the fire when the ammunition hoist broke; as the crew raised the shells hand to hand, on the third shot one of the guns burst but not before scoring a hit on an enemy ship.

Koundouriotis, heartened by the Turks' inaccuracy, altered course to starboard to shorten the range for his own novice gunners, and three minutes later, at a range of some nine miles, the *Averof* fired its own guns for the first time. The first gun bell, the signal to open fire, tinkled in the fore starboard turret, commanded by Sakellariou. The two guns of his turret belched flame while below decks the stokers poured on the coal for extra speed. The entire ship groaned with the strain. Sakellariou and his gun crew coughed in the fumes from the gun breeches, loading and firing like clockwork. Then the right hand gun jammed and Sakellariou spent ten tense minutes taking apart the breech and putting it back together again. Then a gunner cried out: 'Flames on the lead enemy ship!' and set off a cheer that resounded throughout the cruiser. The cruisers *Spetsai*, *Hydra* and *Psara* opened up in support. More enemy shells screamed in, raising more 'cypress trees' of water on either side of the cruiser. Red-hot fragments smacked into the decks and superstructure, shattering wood fittings.

But Koundouriotis became aware of a more serious problem. His older cruisers, capable of just twelve knots, were unable to keep up with the faster *Averof*. But if he reduced speed to match theirs, he wouldn't be able to use his armoured cruiser the way it was meant to be used. The Turkish ships were now just under eight miles away and so far none of them had been seriously damaged, despite a few lucky hits. The Greek admiral was also hobbled by orders not to risk his valuable warship against any sizeable force without support. But how could he face his men if the Turks got off unscathed? The answer was to apply Commander Tsoukalas' audacity doctrine for armoured cruisers: throw the enemy off balance with an aggressive move in his direction. Koundouriotis signalled the *Spetsai*'s skipper to assume temporary command of the fleet. Minutes later the signal flag Z went up the mast – 'Disregard my movements – am acting independently.' Koundouriotis was gambling that he could get between the Turks and their base and hammer them without hindrance. Its smokestacks belching, the *Averof* within twenty minutes had perpendicularly crossed the course of the *Barbaros Hayreddin* – a manoeuvre known as crossing the T – putting it into a position to hurl broadsides at Ramiz's flagship, which could only bring its forward guns to bear. While that was going on, the three older Greek cruisers engaged the attention of the *Turgut Reis*, *Mesudiye* and *Asar-i Tevfik* from the west.

Ramiz, of course, had no intention of remaining in his suddenly-vulnerable position. As the Greek flagship bore down on him he ordered a 180-degree starboard change of course to the southeast, the *Barbaros Hayreddin* to lead and the others to proceed single file in its wake. The message seemed to be clear enough, but true to Tsoukalas' theory, the initial experience of battle seems to have disoriented the commanders of the other cruisers which, instead of following the flagship in line astern, turned in unison. That left

Ramiz's fleet extremely vulnerable to broadside shelling, and the Turkish commander had little choice but to race for the shelter of the Dardanelles, with the *Averof* in hot pursuit. To Lourentzos, observing from the *Hydra*, the *Averof* resembled 'a terrible raging monster ... a colossal Poseidon churning the sea'. The range between the two flagships had closed to about two miles when the Cape Helles shore batteries opened up, pouring murderous fire at the Greeks at just over 5,000 yards.

What followed were tense minutes for Koundouriotis. Shells from Cape Helles and Ramiz's ships came over thick and fast. Two hit the *Averof*'s aft smokestack and the observation port of the aft fire control system, killing a signalman. Another slammed into a lifeboat station directly over Sakellariou's turret. The shock stunned him and his crew and filled the turret with suffocating smoke; Sakellariou reported experiencing 'a terrible pain at the base of my skull and down the nerves of my spine,' with the shock of the explosion. Actually, he seems to have suffered no physical injury. He figured it was a heavy shell from a shore battery, through the thunder of which he could hear the chatter of machine guns. A gunnery sub lieutenant in the port fore turret was seriously wounded in the legs (and died later of his wounds). Five petty officers were also hurt. The shock of the shell bursts ripped wireless cables from their masts and shattered unsecured objects such as thermometers and barometers and washroom fittings. Luckily, most of the Turkish projectiles missed the ship, whose own guns, depressed for the minimum range, threw up great sheets of spray with each salvo so that the range-finding gunnery officer couldn't do his job properly. As the ship turned to follow Ramiz, the port guns had their turn.

Koundouriotis and the ship's commander, Captain Sophocles Dousmanis, descended to the shelter of the lower bridge. All that the men on the other cruisers could see of the *Averof*'s position was a huge moving column of spray and smoke lit up like a flickering neon sign by the gun-flashes. Only the ship's topmasts and battle ensigns were visible. But as it became clear that the Turkish fleet had withdrawn, at about 10.25 am Koundouriotis ordered his gunners to cease fire and gave up the chase. A little later the other cruisers caught up and sailed past, their crews cheering and throwing their hats in the air. Koundouriotis acknowledged them from his position on the lower bridge with a faint smile, saluting the rest of the fleet, eighteen ships in all, as they gathered around the *Averof* like ducklings with their mother.

An initial survey of the damage showed that two shells had penetrated the forward hull, making a mess of some of the seamen's quarters and the map room, all of which miraculously had been unoccupied at the time. Great shell fragments littered the decks. Sakellariou's own turret bore several scars, while some of the armour plating had warped and the rivets had popped.

There was a brief alarm when a ship was spotted coming from the direction of the Kumkale batteries. The destroyer *Nea Genea* was sent to intercept what turned out to be an Italian hospital ship that was on its way to Naples and was approaching the Greek fleet in case it needed any help with casualties. Koundouriotis coldly turned down the offer. He signalled the *Delfin* to see if the sub had accomplished anything, but its skipper replied that strong currents had prevented him from engaging the enemy. The *Averof*'s crew were in the throes of frustration after their battle-high, gulping down their coffee and cursing the fact that not a single Turkish ship had been sunk. The destroyers were kept in place to continue their patrols while the *Averof* returned to its base at Mudros at 10.00 pm. Sakellariou was too keyed up to sleep, so he jumped out of his bunk and paced the foredeck. He was due for the 8.00 pm–to–midnight watch anyway, but then fatigue caught up with him and he began to doze off on his feet. Finally, his watch at an end, he fell into his bunk fully clothed.

The next day Koundouriotis received a signal from a Russian vessel that two listing Turkish cruisers had been seen entering the Dardanelles. An Austrian ship's crew said it saw what looked like a heap of bodies on the deck of one of them, and signs of a 'large explosion' on another. That afternoon the funeral of the luckless signalman of the *Averof* was held on Limnos. It was Sakellariou's first chance to step on *terra firma* in more than two months. Then the congratulations poured in – telegrams from the king and prime minister on down to many private citizens. Sakellariou was showing some visiting army officers around the ship when the sound of cheering erupted from the afterdeck: the destroyer *Nea Genea* had signalled that the *Barbaros Hayreddin* had suffered devastating damage with many casualties.[2]

The battle of Cape Helles was a signal to Turkey's rulers that their navy was in sore need of serious overhaul. Since 16 October the Ottoman navy had been organized in four geographical fleets based in the Bosporus, the Dardanelles and Black Sea. On 19 December, two weeks after the battle, the navy was restructured according to function. The four geographical fleets were replaced by an equal number of functional divisions. The Armoured Warship Division, commanded by Ramiz Bey, comprised the four cruisers that had fought at Cape Helles plus the lighter cruisers *Demirhisar*, *Sultanhisar*, *Sivrihisar* and *Hamidabad*, and the hospital ship *Reshid Pasha*. There were also two destroyer divisions, the First and the Second, commanded by Commodore Hüseyin Rauf Bey and Captain Hakki respectively, totalling nine destroyers. A Third Division comprised smaller and auxiliary vessels under Commander Ismail Bey.

As his fleet licked its wounds at the navy's forward base at Nagara, Ramiz pondered his next move. There seemed only one option open to him: to initiate a fresh action, drawing off the *Averof* by some feint while the bulk of what would soon become the Armoured Warship Division carried out a lightning raid on the main Greek naval station at Mudros. If successful, the operation would restore some measure of control of the northern Aegean to the Ottomans, and delay or even eliminate the military pressure from the Balkan allies overland in Macedonia and Thrace. The next few weeks were taken up with repairing the ships and resting the crews.

Ramiz was not entirely inactive during this period. On 9 December the *Mecidiye* and three destroyers hammered the Greek-held main port of Tenedos but withdrew when the *Averof* hove into view. The Turkish commander moved his flag to the pre-dreadnought *Turgut Reis*, its sister ship *Barbaros Hayreddin* being too badly damaged to serve as a flagship. In the meantime, the controlled Turkish press was telling its readers that the *Averof* had been captured and the red crescent hoisted on it – reports that caused a mixture of fury and amusement when relayed (probably exaggerated in turn by the Greek media) to the crew.

In Athens the government was hatching big plans. Two staff officers called on Koundouriotis on 18 December with instructions from Crown Prince Constantine to explore the possibility of an amphibious army landing on both sides of the Dardanelles. But the strategic equation in the Balkans had suddenly changed. By now the Bulgarians and the Serbs had signed a truce with the Ottomans, who could concentrate all their forces on Greece. With some difficulty Bulgarian forces had been persuaded to quit Thessaloniki, which now was entirely in Greek hands. That only increased Bulgarian enmity, but the Greek government brushed such considerations aside. Bit by bit, in many minds, the old Byzantine Empire was being reclaimed, and that was all that mattered in Athens. The staff officers sailed on a destroyer to reconnoitre the straits. Four days later the *Mecidiye* emerged to chase a few of the Greek destroyers. Koundouriotis received word that the *Hamidiye* had been repaired and was heading down the strait. He braced for another fight, but the Turkish ships scuttled back to their base before he could move. There were several probing sorties like this through December. On New Year's Eve the *Averof*'s wardroom rang with the clinking of glasses and toasts to more victories in 1913.

But while the champagne corks were popping, the Turks were moving. On 2 January the inhabitants of the island of Syros, barely 100 miles from Piraeus in the middle of the Cyclades islands, were jolted awake by the sound of heavy explosions. On the first day of the year the *Hamidiye* had somehow eluded the Greek destroyers guarding the entrance to the strait and raced across the Aegean to shell the ammunition stores on Syros and a recently-converted former passenger ship, the *Makedonia*. A chastened Koundouriotis ordered his destroyers to track down the enemy raider, but a dark and stormy night foiled them. Another Turkish probe emerged on 4 January but withdrew before it could be intercepted. Koundouriotis figured that these moves were feints and refused to be drawn by them.

The purpose of the raid on Syros and other sorties was to lure the *Averof* and escorts out and leave Mudros unguarded. When that didn't happen, Ramiz ordered a surprise attack on the Greek fleet in Mudros Bay. Koundouriotis kept his ships on steam for any eventuality, but Turkish security was good and in the cold, clear morning of 5 January Ramiz set in motion his plan. At dawn the Ottoman seamen assembled at the Nagara base for a solemn event. Before their ranks an honour guard bore a large red flag said to have been used by Hayreddin Barbarossa, the renowned admiral of Sultan Süleyman the Magnificent, the scourge of Christian Europe, whose flag, redolent with golden inscriptions from the Koran, had lain in a museum since the sixteenth century. With great solemnity the oversize flag was hoisted on the foremast of the freshly-repaired *Barbaros Hayreddin* while prayers to Allah to vanquish the aggressive Greeks rose to the clear sky. 'Barbarossa, by defeating the Christian fleets, conquered the whole Mediterranean for the Ottoman Empire,' Ramiz declaimed to his men. 'Your country expects the same from you this day.' (He could not add, of course, that the balance of power in the Mediterranean was now very different!) As the flagship with its big red standard, followed by the *Turgut Reis, Mesudiye, Mecidiye* and the aged *Peyk-i Shevket* brought in from the Suez station, and eight destroyers on their starboard quarter, set out for another crack at the Greek fleet, the spirit of the Ottoman navy was transported back four centuries to the era of the great conquering sultans.

Koundouriotis was not caught napping. Over the Christmas and New Year holidays he had maintained a destroyer patrol schedule around the mouth of the strait. One of the destroyers, the *Leon* – itself invisible to the enemy as it hugged the dark background of the Makronissia islands – spotted Ramiz's fleet as it surged past Cape Helles at about 8.30 am. 'Enemy fleet coming out on course 270,' the *Leon* radioed to Koundouriotis, followed by a brief description of the lineup. There is some confusion, however, about whether the Turks intercepted the messages or not. Some accounts claim that they didn't, though Lourentzos in his short memoir credits Koundouriotis with radioing back to the *Leon:* 'Am far away, cannot help' – if true, a clever piece of deception which the Turks could have swallowed whole. Lourentzos cites the reaction of an ethnic Greek soldier in Ottoman service on board the *Barbaros Hayreddin* who heard that the *Averof* was absent, and feared that the rest of the Greek fleet might be wiped out. Whatever the truth, there can be no doubt that Ramiz's exodus was compromised almost from the beginning. But to him and his captains, the western sea horizon was refreshingly clear; a few hours' steady steaming and they would pounce on the Greeks at Mudros.

On receiving the signal from the *Leon* Koundouriotis let his crew have a leisurely breakfast before sounding battle stations for his fleet: 'Enemy fleet approaching from thirty miles east. Prepare for immediate sailing. Everything depends on today. Be lions.' The sea was mill-pond calm and by 10.15 am the *Averof* had got up steam and was clearing Cape Irini with the *Spetsai, Hydra* and *Psara* in its wake, the destroyers screening the cruisers on either side. The sight of them disconcerted Ramiz, who probably realized at this point that he had already lost his gamble on surprise. The Turkish commander now had no choice but to fight it out in the open sea, far from the shelter of the Dardanelles, on terms no better for him than in the battle of Cape Helles a month before.

Koundouriotis and Ramiz stalked each other cautiously, the former keeping his ships at full speed on a south-easterly course, the latter heading southwest at a convergent angle. Koundouriotis aimed to cut off Ramiz's advance in another crossing of the T, forcing him to turn and get the sun in his eyes. By now Barbarossa's great red flag was clearly visible to the Greeks, who puzzled over it. The *Mecidiye* had been in the process of chasing a couple of Greek destroyers when it caught sight of the main Greek force and steered back into its original position. At about 11.45 am, when the opposing fleets were some eight miles apart, the *Averof*'s port guns loosed their first salvo, followed by a fast rate of fire. Ramiz's ships returned an equally furious fire, but their aim was poor. 'Haven't they learned how to use their guns yet?' the *Averof*'s crew scoffed as the enemy shells plopped harmlessly into the sea. For some ninety minutes the guns of both sides belched unceasingly but, as at Cape Helles, the Greeks' fast, flat fire was too much for their adversaries and Ramiz ordered his damaged fleet to turn for the strait.

During the turn the *Mesudiye* caught heavy punishment, while its sister cruisers, appearing to repeat their mistake of 3 December, broke formation in some confusion. And, as on the previous occasion, it was the *Averof* that pursued the Turks north-eastwards, leaving the slower Greek ships behind. This time, however, Koundouriotis knew that if he kept on his present course keeping the Turks to starboard he would run into an extensive shoal off the east side of Limnos, known appropriately as Death Reef, so he altered course slightly, weaving some five miles behind the retreating Turkish fleet, maintaining fire alternately from port to starboard. Sakellariou reported seeing 'an enormous standard' on the enemy flagship (which he mistakenly took to be the *Turgut Reis*); this must have been Barbarossa's 400-year-old flag which, as he watched, vanished in a great orange fireball. Sakellariou's crew got their chance to fire at 1.30 pm, sometimes without bothering to wait for the tinkle of the firing bell, which earned him several reprimands from the bridge.

Ramiz was not about to repeat the mistake of Cape Helles and get himself into another scrap with the *Averof.* He knew the Greek commander would try and cut off his fleet's retreat, so to cut his losses he ordered an immediate course for home. The Turkish fleet stopped firing as soon as it reached the protection of the Kumkale shore batteries at 2.35 pm, outrunning the *Averof* which was juddering flat out at its maximum twenty-three knots. At the entrance to the strait the *Mesudiye*, though seriously damaged, stopped to cover the retreat with a few ineffective shots. Wreathed in smoke from the fires and smokestacks, the battered Ottoman fleet vanished up the strait. To Lourentzos watching from the *Hydra*, it appeared as if the *Averof* 'was standing and glaring at the enemy and saying, "You fleeing cowards!"' Koundouriotis ordered the *Averof*'s band to assemble on deck and play, while the cheers of the crew drowned out the occasional ineffective blast from the shore batteries.

Sakellariou went up to the bridge to find Koundouriotis looking concerned. An enemy shell had bounced off the base of the fore port turret, pierced the deck and exploded in the fortunately empty sick bay, pulverizing it. Fragments had smashed water lines, flooding some compartments including the switchboard and giving the ship a list of some two degrees to port. A second shell had exploded in the same general area. The whole front of the *Averof* was wreathed in smoke from the resulting fires, which were brought under control by the time the ship returned to Mudros. On the floor of the shattered sick bay Sakellariou found part of the shell's detonator, which he kept as a souvenir of the battle of Limnos.

Incredibly, there were no fatalities on the Greek side. The *Averof*'s sole casualty was an able seaman who was wounded by the shell that devastated the sick bay; he had inadvertently locked himself outside the bay's armoured doors, a mistake that saved his life. Turkish casualties this time were quite heavy: some 500, of which half were fatalities, including the captain of the *Barbaros Hayreddin*, Captain Enver Hakki. The *Asar-i Tevfik* ran aground and capsized. Part of the Greeks' success, apart from the undoubted skills and seamanship of Rear Admiral Koundouriotis, can be put down to the quality of the *Averof*'s armour and superiority of its Vickers guns. The inaccuracy of the Turks' gunfire also played a part; in the entire five-hour engagement the *Averof* sustained just two direct hits. The guns of the *Barbaros Hayreddin* and *Turgut Reis* may have been heavier, but their muzzle velocities fell far short of the *Averof*'s. The Turkish shore batteries at Kumkale could not help much, as they were high-trajectory, which in a sea battle was a distinct disadvantage compared to the flat, fast fire of the Greek ships. Finally, there was the sheer luck which would cloak itself like a protecting force field round the *Averof* for the rest of its long career. It was probably at this point that the ship earned the nickname Lucky Uncle George. Yet infinitely more damaging to the Turks than the *Averof*'s gunfire – more than 600 shells in a couple of hours – was the morale of the Ottoman navy after Limnos. The battle at one stroke ended the Ottoman Empire's effective sea power and sealed Greece's European domination of the Aegean Sea and islands. Well might Marshal Hüseyin Nazim (Pasha), the Ottoman chief of staff, lament in an official report: 'The fleet has done all it can and nothing further can be expected ...' Captain Ramiz Bey was court-martialled and cashiered.

The enthusiasm on the Greek side was correspondingly booming. Katsouros the engineer, brimming with the feverish Crusader-era bombast that had perniciously and thoroughly infected both sides, jotted in his diary:

Again the Cross has triumphed over the half moon, and yet another page of glory has been added to Greece's naval history.

The battle made an overpowering impression on Lourentzos as 'a most magnificent, moving but also terrible spectacle which no [ordinary] man is likely to encounter in his lifetime'. As with the previous battle of Cape Helles, officialdom was fulsome in its praise. King George I cabled a terse two-line congratulation to the crew of the *Averof*. (It was of the king's last official acts, as he was assassinated two months later.) Nikolaos Stratos, the navy minister, 'could not find words' to express his own emotions. But when the ministry demanded an immediate report on the movements of the opposing fleets, damage and casualties, Koundouriotis, having been under intense strain, cabled back: 'I gave you victory and that should suffice for now!'

From that moment the Turkish navy ceased to be a sea power of any consequence. The twin defeats at Cape Helles and Limnos shocked the Ottoman government into toying with the idea of peace terms. Within the space of a month it had completely lost control of the northern Aegean, rendering it unable to resupply its remaining forces in the Balkan peninsula and hastening the end of the First Balkan War. Rumours that the government was about to cede European territory to Bulgaria triggered a violent reaction among the ultra-militant CUP; less than three weeks after the battle of Limnos extremists burst into the cabinet room and shot dead Marshal Nazim, who in addition to chief of staff held the post of war minister. But even the militants had to accept reality; there was no way the Balkan clock could be turned back now. Besides, there were powerful forces in Turkey itself – not least in the armed forces – that pressed for a modernization of the country and its eventual acceptance into the law-abiding community of nations.

The sultan's emissaries signed a truce with the Balkan allies on 31 March 1913, ratified by the Treaty of London at the end of May. The treaty's main features confirmed the Aegean Sea and the great majority of its islands as an area of Greek sovereignty, backed by a guarantee of the Great Powers. The Ottoman Empire also relinquished its claims to Crete, opening the way for the island's formal union with Greece. In Turkey the resulting humiliation only hardened the stand of the CUP-controlled governments, who inaugurated a period of dictatorship that lasted through the First World War and beyond. Hüseyin Rauf (Bey), the only senior naval officer to score any tactical success at sea during the First Balkan War, was rewarded with senior political positions which he occupied until his death in 1964.

Koundouriotis gained plenty of intelligence about the state of the Ottoman fleet through ethnic Greek deserters and the cloak-and-dagger efforts of Lieutenant Antonios Kriezis, a former naval attaché to Constantinople, who returned to the city under cover and counted at least sixty large shell holes in the Turkish ships. Kriezis also reported that much of the *Turgut Reis* had been smashed, as well as half the big guns of the *Mesudiye*. But the admiral couldn't afford to relax his vigilance. From his base at Mudros he kept his ships stoked and steamed, ready for immediate action. More than once Lucky Uncle George and the other cruisers hurriedly weighed anchor on reports that Turkish warships were emerging from the straits, but the alarms turned out to be false. The cold at Mudros was bitter. 'We're frozen to death,' Sakellariou confided to his diary on 17 February. 'A blizzard came today and you couldn't stand upright on the deck. There was danger from chunks of ice that the wind broke off the masts and cables.' A week later the Mudros port officer was married to his sweetheart on board the *Averof*. In the middle of the wedding service the alarm sounded – enemy ships exiting the strait! The chaplain hurried the ceremony to a patched-up conclusion as the crew scattered to get the ship underway. This alarm, like all the others, was a dud. (In fact, it might well have been a practical joke on the port officer, whose main concern, according to Sakellariou, was to boast to everyone how pretty his bride looked!)

Yet a threat of sorts did remain, and that was the coastal defence cruiser *Hamidiye*, reported to have been repaired and coaled at Port Said and ready for action again. In mid-January it had been sighted at Malta, then reported to be on its way to Beirut. As a nervous navy ministry in Athens bombarded Koundouriotis with what-are-you-doing-about-it? cables, the admiral despatched the destroyers *Velos* and *Nike* to check out the story, which turned out to have been deliberately planted by the Turks, for on 28 February the *Hamidiye* turned up hundreds of miles away, off the Albanian port of Dürres, shelling the town and some Serbian troopships. The Serbs set up some field artillery pieces on the ships and fired back at four miles, forcing the *Hamidiye* to withdraw.

Koundouriotis ordered the cruiser *Psara* and a destroyer into the Adriatic to intercept the *Hamidiye,* but the Ottoman cruiser eluded them and arrived at Alexandria, having sunk a Greek freighter on the way. On 24 March the *Hamidiye* traversed the Suez Canal and dropped anchor at Ismailiya while the RHN cruiser *Hydra,* accompanied by the destroyers *Keravnos* and *Doxa,* stalked it four miles off Port Said. A week later the Treaty of London was signed, the First Balkan War over, and the ships returned to base. The Greeks, meanwhile, were trying to get over the shock of the assassination of venerable King George I, shot dead by a deranged man while taking a stroll in newly-Greek Thessaloniki. By that time the king's son and successor, Constantine I, had regained Epiros for Greece and the Balkan frontiers appeared to be on the way to stabilization.

The crew of the *Averof* erupted in cheers when the suspension of hostilities with Turkey was announced. It was not music to Koundouriotis' ears, and he ordered it stopped. 'It does not become brave men,' he said, 'to cheer for peace!' The outburst (recorded by Sakellariou) says a great deal about Koundouriotis' temperament, and perhaps more about the spirit of the times. His command of the RHN in the Aegean had been the most important and exciting period of his entire career. The victories at Cape Helles and Limnos were more in the way of achievement than any of his rank had a right to expect in such a short time. He believed that in the *Averof* he had the equivalent of Hephaistos' magic shield described in Homer's *Iliad*, the great metallic mojo that would establish Greek hegemony in the Aegean and Asia Minor forever. The ship was still quite new, and he wanted to do more with it. He thought in Spartan terms; peace was for cowards. Besides, the whole of Greece was aflame with an irredentist chauvinism that may seem excessive from the vantage point of a century on, but was the very essence of patriotism at the time, and lingers still today. No senior officer, even if he privately felt otherwise, could go against the grain.

The Aegean fleet remained on alert to meet a possible Bulgarian threat, while repairs to battle damage were made. On 20 May the *Averof* and its sister ships made a triumphant entry into the port of Thessaloniki, the Greek flag now flying from the city's landmark White Tower. Scenes from the islands replayed themselves, as boatloads of enthusiastic Thessalonians thronged the sea around Lucky Uncle George. Koundouriotis was mobbed wherever he went. Venizelos, the prime minister, came on board, but Sakellariou noted that he 'looked a lot older' since his last visit to the ship nine months before. The war had aged him.

The high ceremonial aspect of Balkan power struggles on the eve of the First World War never ceased to dominate life on board the *Averof*. The day after its arrival at Thessaloniki was Saint Constantine's Day, the nameday of King Constantine I. To the Greeks until quite recently, the nameday was far more important than the birthday as an occasion for partying and putting on one's best clothes. The solemnity reached its peak as the king attended a service at the city cathedral – the first time a Greek monarch had set foot there for at least 500 years – amid stiff ranks of soldiers and sailors beneath the elaborate icons and standards of the Orthodox Church, as the incense wafted on the air and the ancient tones of the Byzantine liturgy echoed off the ornate Ottoman-era buildings. The evocation of the vanished Byzantine Empire was quite deliberate, as many Greeks in high places – not to mention a large majority of RHN and army officers – were under the heady but tragically misguided impression that with God's help they were about to resurrect the thousand-year glory of Greek Constantinople.

With the official cessation of the First Balkan War in June, the state of blockade of the Dardanelles was lifted, and the *Averof* returned to its base at Mudros. But the successes of the war had whetted the irredentists' appetite for more. With the Ottomans out of the way it was the turn now of the Slavs of Bulgaria to feel the heat of Greek territorial demands. Though Greece and Bulgaria had been uneasy allies during the war, it was a moot point who cut the worse figure in the Greek popular imagination, Turk or Bulgar. The Greek political establishment was obsessed by the fear that a new, strong Bulgaria would muscle its way towards an outlet on the warm Mediterranean, trampling on ethnic Greek populations in Macedonia and Thrace. It was not an irrational fear, as Bulgarian nationalist societies were aiming at precisely that. Bulgaria and Serbia had patched up their own territorial issues in February 1912; a similar deal between Greece and Bulgaria in May 1912 had left wide open the question of what to do with ex-Ottoman lands in Europe. By the time the *Averof* and its sister ships were making history at sea, the last phase of the Balkan War had become a race between Greece and Bulgaria for how much territory their soldiers could control. The Bulgarians had received a slap in the face in October when the Greeks beat them to Thessaloniki and allowed entry to only a few of the Bulgarian detachments who had also fought in the campaign.

The Ottomans enjoyed brief encouragement that summer, when Greece and Bulgaria fell out over the Balkan spoils. When Serbia attacked Bulgaria from the north and west, Bulgaria asked for a truce. Venizelos, the Greek prime minister, wisely agreed as in the meantime Ottoman forces had taken advantage of the Greek-Bulgarian scrap and had reoccupied some of their European lands around Edirne. The resulting Treaty of Bucharest delineated what still remain the frontiers of Greece, Turkey and Bulgaria, but left unresolved the ethnic and religious quarrels that plagued Serbia and its neighbours such as Bosnia-Herzegovina and Montenegro. Those quarrels, within a year, would ignite the greatest war the world had yet seen.

Skirmishes between Greek and Bulgarian troops had occurred as early as February 1913. As Bulgaria massed troops on the Greek border, Greece and Serbia inked a protocol of military cooperation. A Russian attempt at mediation failed, and on 16 June Bulgarian forces attacked the Greeks, triggering the brief Second Balkan War. King Constantine I responded by ordering the Bulgarian garrison out of Thessaloniki. The garrison refused to move, so the Greek 2nd Division stormed it, capturing its survivors after an all-night street battle. Maintaining the initiative, the 2nd, 3rd, 4th and 5th Divisions moved into the Kilkis area, while the 1st and 6th advanced on Lahana. Sharp battles took place at both locations, resulting in Greek victories, though at considerable cost in casualties.

Kavala, a key north Aegean port, fell on 15 June, easing the position of the RHN, with other towns following suit. A Bulgarian counterattack at Petsovo on 15 July stopped and drove back the Greek 7th Division that had penetrated well into Bulgaria along the Nestos River Valley. This was followed by a concerted attack on the Greek 3rd and 10th Divisions which were hard pressed to keep their positions. But the Bulgarian offensive suddenly weakened, as the Serbian Third Army attacked Bulgaria from the west. The war was well on its way to a bloody stalemate when an unexpected Turkish incursion into Thrace collected Balkan minds, and on 28 October 1913 the Second Balkan War drew to a close with the Treaty of Bucharest defining the frontiers of Greece, Serbia, Bulgaria and what was left of the Ottoman Empire in Europe.

Judging from his curmudgeonly reaction to the cessation of hostilities of the First Balkan War, Koundouriotis would have been glad at the new scrap. He had about as much use for the Bulgarians as the Turks, which wasn't very much. When the new war was

The *Averof* shortly after commissioning.

RHNS *Averof* under construction at Livorno, 1909.

Admiral Pavlos
Koundouriotis

Launch of the *Averof* at Livorno,
12 March 1910.

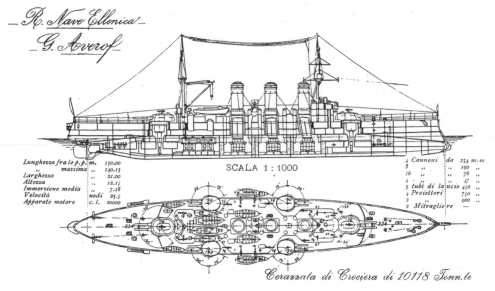

R. Nave Ellenica
G. Averof

SCALA 1 : 1000

Lunghezza fra le p.p.	m.	130.00
" massima	"	140.13
Larghezza	"	21.00
Altezza	"	12.15
Immersione media	"	7.18
Velocità	nodi	23.5
Apparato motore	c.l.	20000

4	Cannoni	da	234	m/m
8	"	"	190	"
16	"	"	76	"
4	"	"	47	"
3	tubi di lancio	450	"
4	Proiettori	750	"
2		900	—
2	Mitragliere	—

Corazzata di Crociera di 10118 Tonn.te

Invitation to the launching ceremony, featuring the basic ship plan.

The _Averof_ dry-docked at Portsmouth after its
accident, 1911.

Orlando Bros. nameplate on the _Averof._

The *Averof* and fleet leave Phaleron Bay for operations in the Aegean, 5 October 1912.

Captain Dousmanis at the stern.

The *Averof*'s crew at Mudros, late 1912.

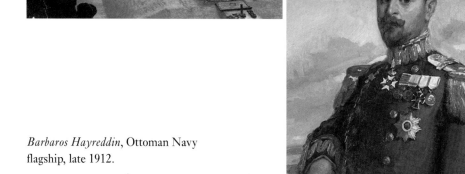

The First Balkan War at sea.

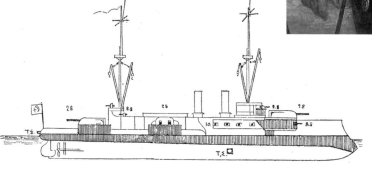

Barbaros Hayreddin, Ottoman Navy
flagship, late 1912.

Dousmanis.

Hamidiye,
Ottoman Navy
armoured
cruiser.

Contemporary painting of the Battle of Cape Helles, December 1912, by S. Plytas.

Contemporary painting of the Battle of Limnos, January 1913, by C. Alexandris.

The *Averof* leads the fleet on exercises (c. 1920).

Admiral Koundouriotis' quarters (restored).

The captain's cabin (restored).

The captain's bathroom (restored).

Inside the closed bridge.

The open and closed bridge.

Officers' dining room
(restored).

Officers' lounge
(restored).

Ship's chapel.

'Saint' image on the
powder bucket.

Balkan Wars naval uniforms. Left to right: Lieutenant, Chief Petty Officer, Lieutenant Commander.

More naval uniforms. Left to right: Able Seaman, Captain, Admiral.

Stern view of the *Averof* today.

View of the afterdeck.

Aft guns.

Port aft gun turret.

Port fore gun turrent.

Capstan with Orlando Bros. insignia.

Aft smokestack.

View of the foredeck.

Fore guns.

Shrapnel damage on
a gun barrel from the
Battle of Cape Helles.

Fire control post from
1925 refit.

Vintage 1912 rangefinder.

Main kitchen.

Sick bay kitchen.

The armoury.

Crew's hammocks (restored).

A wooden cross brought out by the ship's chaplain in times of danger to encourage the crew.

Canvas slings for loading coal down the chutes.

Stoker's uniform, Balkan Wars era.

The Ansaldo triple-expansion engine.

View of the engine room.

Boiler pressure gauges.

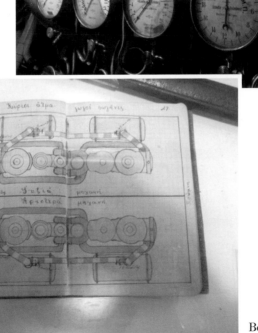

Boiler diagram for
engine room crew.

Rear Admiral Alexander Sakellariou.

The *Averof* in the Indian Ocean, 1941–42.

Docked at Bombay, 1941.

HNS *Velos*, moored
alongside the *Averof*, today.

declared on 17 June, Koundouriotis ordered the Aegean fleet to patrol off the northern shore. The *Averof* lobbed a few shells inland at ancient Amphipolis where Bulgarian units were believed to be; the destroyer *Leon* bombarded a Bulgarian camp nearby. But this was now almost exclusively a land war, and the frustrated crews felt it keenly, especially when reports emerged of alleged Bulgarian atrocities. The most that the *Averof* and other ships could do was cruise back and forth along the coast east of Thessaloniki enforcing a blockade and hoping to intimidate the enemy by the sight of masses of floating metal. On two occasions salvoes were fired at Bulgarian army positions near the coast because as Sakellariou, for one, fretted, 'there was no Bulgarian navy' for them to get at!

On 25 June Koundouriotis saw his chance for more glory. Closely following the progress of operations on land, when Kavala was about to fall he offered to steam to that port with a force of marines and claim it for Greece. The General Staff declined his request for troops, but ordered the destroyer *Doxa* to do the job, which it did the following day. On 6 July the navy ministry in Athens took the destroyers *Nea Genea* and *Lonchi* off their patrols at the entrance to the Dardanelles, judging that there was no longer a danger from that quarter. Later that month the British naval attaché came on board the *Averof* and, if we are to credit Sakellariou, exclaimed in wonder at Koundouriotis' exposition of the battles of Cape Helles and Limnos, claiming that the Admiralty in London hadn't really been aware of them!

Bulgarian forces abandoned Dedeagach (Alexandroupolis) on 11 July and the *Averof* duly steamed there to make its presence felt and reassure the nervous Greek populace that the motherland wouldn't abandon them. Engine room personnel made themselves useful repairing a couple of Turkish locomotives damaged by the retreating Bulgarians. By this time, peace feelers were well under way. When it appeared certain that an armistice would be signed, King Constantine ordered the *Averof* to fire a 101-gun salute and issued a proclamation that unabashedly spoke of 'a Greece respected by her friends and terrible to her foes.'

Such naive bombast was considered quite normal, nay desirable, at the time. It was an era of sabre-rattling around the globe. Nations such as Greece, with less than a century of modern statehood behind them, needed to assert an aggressive identity to survive in the new, ironclad twentieth century world. Nowhere was this truer – and it's still true – in the Balkans, where ethnic and religious rivalries and hatreds went back a very long time, perpetuated by poverty and the touchy emotional characteristics of the peoples themselves. It is safe to say that not one man on the *Averof*, for example, failed to share the overwhelming and emotional nationalism that had given them a new lease on life. The Greeks' military achievements in the Balkan wars had raised the eyebrows of no less a ruler than Kaiser Wilhelm II – the same Wilhelm who in less than a year would help plunge Europe into its greatest bloodbath – who awarded the rank of field marshal to his brother-in-law Constantine I.

Constantine himself lost no chance to visit the armoured cruiser that had given his country victory. The following days for the *Averof* were a dizzying round of visits to Thessaloniki and other ports, a kaleidoscope of cheering crowds, pomp and royal circumstance, champagne parties for plumed and epauletted officers and officials, fire-breathing speeches and *te deum* services in the Orthodox churches. The *Averof* with the king on board and the Aegean fleet returned to its home base at Phaleron Bay on 4 August, the shore batteries lining the Attic coast booming in welcome. Technically the fleet remained on the alert, as peace negotiations with the Ottoman Empire and the Balkan powers see-sawed between progress and setback. Only with the official signing of the peace on 1 November could Koundouriotis and his crew finally relax, and the great ship settle down for a well-deserved rest. It was in several ways Greece's finest hour. In a few years it had almost doubled its territory and equipped itself with the most formidable navy in southeast Europe. There was every reason to believe that Greece was on its way to becoming the dominant power in that region.

Chapter 6

Sailing to Byzantium

So therefore I have sailed the seas and come
To the holy city of Byzantium.

William Butler Yeats

Approaching Istanbul by sea from the south is, even now, an unforgettable experience. The shores of the Sea of Marmara slowly narrow, and at their apex there rises the great dome of Sancta Sophia and its Ottoman-era minarets, like an artificial sun against the blue-grey sky. As the voyager closes in on Seraglio Point, the great city surges up from the horizon, high-rise offices and hotels vying with the great mosques and sultans' palaces. The waterside roads are thick with speeding traffic; buses and taxis and pedestrians throng the bridge over the entrance to the Golden Horn. Ferries and tankers and cruise ships jostle for priority in the rushing current of the Bosporus. The sheer living, pulsing presence of a 2,700-year-old metropolis, the seat of empires, the commercial and strategic nexus of two continents, is as indefinable as it is overwhelming.

In 1919 the world still called it Constantinople, even under the Ottomans. And to the crew of the *Averof,* as it steamed grandly up to the defeated Turkish capital, it seemed as if the very pages of history were turning: the Cathedral City, the symbol of Greek Byzantine power for 1,000 years, the dream of patriotic poets, teachers, writers and politicians and priests for 500 more, was finally back in the national bosom. Yes, those defacing infidel minarets would soon be swept from the corners of Sancta Sophia; the Orthodox chants would echo in there again, the blue and white flag would fly over the waters of the Bosporus, the Turk would at last be pulled down from his high horse. But it wasn't going to happen.

The reason was the First World War, which meanwhile had upset the entire European and Middle Eastern balances of power. Greece had been spared most of the war's effects. At the outbreak of war in 1914 the country had remained neutral, though King Constantine naturally leaned towards his brother-in-law the Kaiser. To be fair to the king, however, he also had Greece's interests at heart; he had personally led the army to victory in the Balkan Wars and in his view, now was not the time for another upheaval so soon after the last one. But this stand was not to the liking of Venizelos, a staunchly pro-Entente statesman and the country's leading politician, now out of power. Domestic tensions between royalists and liberal 'Venizelists' erupted in violence in 1916, with royalist troops firing on British and French forces that had landed at Piraeus to keep Greece from joining the Central Powers. Forgotten were the days, just a few years before, when king and prime minister would stand together on the deck of the *Averof* and dream of greatness to come. The two men were now sworn enemies. But Venizelos (aided openly by British agents) had the bulk of public opinion with him and felt strong enough in November 1916 to form a separate pro-Entente government based in Thessaloniki. The split was complete.

Admiral Koundouriotis from the first had staunchly supported the Entente and Venizelos, and carried most of the navy establishment with him. Both men nursed hopes that the British and French after the war would give the Greeks a reward for wartime cooperation by helping them reclaim ancient Greek lands in Asia Minor, including Constantinople. Part of Greece's early neutrality, one suspects, was intended to preserve Greek military strength for that devoutly-to-be-wished showdown. The Balkan wars had been merely the first round. Concern increased when Turkey, still under the control of the Young Turk movement, entered the lists on the side of the Central Powers. This meant that if the Central Powers should lose the war, Constantinople and the Bosporus would come under British and Russian control.

The immediate result of all this was that the Royal Hellenic Navy, the mistress of the Aegean, was forced to be a mere spectator while other, stronger navies handled hostilities in the Mediterranean. And nowhere was this more frustratingly apparent than when, in the opening days of the war, the German naval commander in the Mediterranean, Admiral Wilhelm Souchon, received orders to take the two ships under his command, the battlecruiser *Goeben* and light cruiser *Breslau*, to shelter temporarily at Constantinople. Though the order was soon rescinded, Souchon decided to make for the Ottoman capital anyway to escape encirclement by British and French ships. From the sea off Tunis, where he had received the signals, he steamed full speed for the Dardanelles. 'No other single exploit of the war,' noted one of its leading historians, 'cast so long a shadow upon the world' as the dramatic chase of the *Goeben* and *Breslau* through Greek waters.[1] Those fast ships were a serious threat to the French Mediterranean fleet. Hours before war was declared, Winston Churchill as First Lord of the Admiralty ordered HMS *Indomitable* and *Indefatigable* to keep a tight tail on them. Souchon poured on the coal to escape, at the cost of four crewmen scalded to death by bursting boilers. The Turks, meanwhile, had given permission for his ships to pass through the minefields guarding the entrance to the Dardanelles. The Royal Navy squadron under Admiral Sir Ernest Troubridge was hard put to keep them in its sights.

Troubridge badly bungled his mission to bring the two German warships to heel. Neither he nor Churchill appeared to be aware of the ships' true destination; they laboured under the impression that the ships were playing hide-and-seek and would soon swing back to the west where the main action was. Added to this misunderstanding were blunders by Admiralty signallers which halted the commander of the British Mediterranean fleet, Admiral Sir Berkeley Milne, in mid-chase between Malta and Greece. When the mistake was finally corrected on 7 August, the *Goeben* and *Breslau* had vanished around the southern tip of Greece and entered the Aegean with a forty-hour head start.

Koundouriotis had kept up with the dramatic news, and when the *Goeben* and *Breslau* entered Greek waters off Zakynthos he wanted to give chase, but there was one major snag: Greece was officially neutral, a point made bluntly by Rear Admiral Troubridge.

'Then let me lead some British cruisers,' the excitable Koundouriotis pleaded.

'What would your government say?' Troubridge said.

'I don't give a damn for neutrality or the government!' the Greek snapped. 'Say the word and I'll lead the way.'

Koundouriotis was not just being naively bellicose. He had a definite agenda, and that was to help Venizelos steer Greece in Britain's direction. To attack the German ships would go far to qualify the Greek navy for a British alliance. No-one knew the byways of the Aegean like he did. But it was too early to go against the king, and his offer was politely declined. Yet it is worth speculating whether the *Averof* might have stopped the two German ships while they were threading their way through the Aegean islands to safety.

Milne was under the somewhat weird impression that the Aegean was a closed sea, a dead end, into which he could pursue the *Goeben* and *Breslau* at his leisure; it never seems to have occurred to him that

Constantinople was their destination, and that the pursuit would have to stop at the Dardanelles. On 10 August the two ships, waiting in the same waters where the *Averof* had smashed the Ottoman fleet less than two years before, received permission to go through the strait.

Churchill fumed. Turkey was still technically neutral, and the acceptance of the German warships for shelter was an egregious violation of that status. But the Turkish government knew what it was doing. It had no love lost for either Churchill or the Royal Navy since earlier that summer, when Turkish crews had been ready to travel to Barrow-in-Furness and Newcastle to take delivery of two grand new dreadnoughts, the *Sultan Mehmet Reshad* (known also as *Reshadiye*) and the *Sultan Osman-i Evel*. This latter was a super dreadnought, massively long and menacingly low in the water. The funds had been contributed by thousands of ordinary Turks high and low, 'every clerk, blacksmith, dressmaker and goatherd,' in a remarkable outburst of public-spiritedness. Therefore one can imagine the bitterness all Turks felt when Churchill froze the handover. The Turkish crews languished on their rusty transport at Elswick, not even allowed to board their new ship.

Injury was added to insult when Churchill requisitioned the two dreadnoughts, renaming them HMS *Erin* and *Agincourt*. His Majesty's government offered the sultan a paltry £1,000 a day for use of the ships. The Ottoman government, mortally affronted, refused. Churchill may have had cogent strategic reasons for not allowing the newest products of Britain's shipbuilding industry to reach the Turks. But the fact remains that it was a neat piece of chicanery, not far removed from outright theft. More than anything else, it helped push the Turks straight into the arms of Germany, with devastating results for Britain and Churchill at Gallipoli a year later. It also played straight into the hands of Souchon, who offered the *Goeben* and *Breslau* to the Ottoman government which renamed them *Yavuz Sultan Selim* and *Midilli* respectively – another setback for the Entente at sea. And Souchon, in almost a Gilbert and Sullivan parody, was made ruler of the sultan's navy, complete with frock coat and fez.

Koundouriotis, meanwhile, had not been inactive. Unable to lead the *Averof* to more victories, he delved into high-level politics instead. In 1917 he became one of a triumvirate (including Venizelos and an army general) running the pro-Entente separatist government in Thessaloniki. Naturally, the bulk of the RHN went with him. British and French pressure then forced Constantine into exile, and Venizelos returned to Athens in triumph. During that period the *Averof* had remained at Salamis, nosing occasionally into the open sea for gunnery exercises, one of which took place at its old anchorage of Mudros. Thirteen days before the armistice, on 30 October 1918, Turkey threw in the towel. A few months were to pass in minesweeping and wreckage-clearing operations in the Dardanelles before the *Averof* could sail grandly up to Constantinople, where it docked for a few weeks in January 1919, its pennants flying, as the victorious allied powers dismembered the Ottoman Empire. Meanwhile, ordinary Turks sullenly viewed the Greek armoured cruiser – the very symbol of their arch-foe – sitting pretty in the Bosporus entrance along with other allied ships, and muttered revenge. They would soon get it.

The few years after the First World War were a time of shameless land-grabbing by the victorious powers which cynically ignored the idealistic calls of US President Woodrow Wilson for an equitable peace settlement that would hopefully remove the triggers of future wars. Britain and France, each for their own reasons, were determined to hold on to their empires. In the Middle East both were given League of Nations mandates which technically were lands and nations needing the supposed guiding hand of a 'mature' Western power before being allowed independence. The mandates were merely the old colonialism under a politically-correct name. The defunct Ottoman Empire, too, had to be under some kind of Western control, not least because it would help secure Britain's vital connection to India, a link that would obsess Churchill for decades. Greece also wanted its pound of flesh.

Italy had made no secret of its desire to annex some of the eastern Aegean seaboard, which brought it into direct conflict with Greek designs on the same region. Venizelos was, moreover, in a hurry, as Turkish nationalists under General Mustafa Kemal had formed a revolutionary government at Ankara and were massing considerable forces to reclaim the entire Turkish mainland. David Lloyd George, the British prime minister, was also worried. Better the Greeks in Smyrna, he figured, than a hostile Turkish regime. Thanks to Venizelos' vigorous lobbying in Europe's capitals, and over strong French opposition, Greece was awarded the region of Smyrna and its hinterland. It was just a step from there to the fatal Greek misstep of landing troops at Smyrna on 2 May 1919. And the *Averof* was there to support the landings.

It was a grand time to be a Greek in the great Levantine commercial city of Smyrna, especially as the Greeks controlled the great bulk of trade, industry and banking. Almost from the moment the Greek forces arrived, at 7.50 am on 2 May, they were feted and worshipped. The *Averof*'s crew enjoyed its share of the adulation. Greek flags fluttered from balconies everywhere. Officers on shore leave were the guests of honour in countless posh drawing rooms and salons; officers and enlisted men alike were swamped with offers of marriage to local damsels. The poorer Turkish majority envied the status of *Giavur Izmir* – Infidel Smyrna – as the dominant Greek community of some 200,000 people was called. Greek colleges and journals flourished. Recording studios turned out Greek hits on thick precursors of vinyl discs. To all intents and purposes, the Greek and European quarters of Smyrna were a tiny vital corner of Europe in the dying Ottoman Empire.

The *Averof*'s crew would frequent the *Quai,* or waterfront, where men and women paraded the latest fashions in the evenings and seamen could gaze entranced in the windows of department stores and smart cafés. The English Dock, Foti's Café and the Jardin des Fleurs were favourite watering-holes, while hospitable well-to-do families would invite servicemen on coach rides to the Bournova resort. The place where every naval officer had to be seen *de rigueur* was the Sporting Club, a vast, ornate white palace facing the sea, the haunt of industrialists and diplomats. And, as if to remind everyone that the Greek homeland now had sinews of steel, the long grey shape of the *Averof* stood in the water, thin wisps of smoke climbing from its smokestacks, its great guns pointing away over the rooftops of Smyrna in the direction of the Turkish hinterland. If the Byzantine Empire could be reborn, Smyrna in 1920 was what it would have looked like.

The dream was all too brief. The sad story of Greece's defeat in Asia Minor would be outside the scope of this book. Suffice it to say that Mustafa Kemal's brilliant generalship combined with incompetence on the Greek side determined the outcome. The Greeks at first advanced far beyond the presumed limits of Smyrna, and far outside the limits of military sense. King Constantine was aware of the looming strategic problem, but somehow events escaped his control. 'Onward to Ankara!' boomed the jingoist press, creating its own momentum. But Greece's generals were by no means up to such a grandiose aim; their commander-in-chief, in fact, was seriously mentally unbalanced. The *Averof* played a minor part in the war by shelling Samsun on the Black Sea coast in May

1922, moving back to the Aegean to bombard Turkish positions on the coast in September. But this war, again, was very much an army show. Greek planning was not of the best, and inevitably the advancing Greek line became longer and more vulnerable. Kemal judged his counterattack cleverly, and at the Sakarya River halted the Greek advance and turned it into a rout. Appalling atrocities were committed by both sides. The tragic climax occurred in Smyrna on 27 August 1922. The smart waterfront that until then had been the apex of civilized life in the Levant was turned into a blazing mass fronted by panicky crowds trying to get on whatever could float to escape. Advancing Turkish cavalry had set fire to the Christian quarters and the blaze had spread. Thousands of once-well-to-do Greeks found themselves on ships without a penny and with only the clothes on their backs, fleeing across the Aegean to Greece. Countless others perished in the flames or at Turkish hands. Eventually, more than a million ethnic Greeks were driven from Turkey. Far from the greater Greece they had dreamed about, Greece's leaders were now stuck with international humiliation and an intractable refugee problem that would absorb the whole nation's energies for years to come.

The disastrous outcome of the Asia Minor war shook the Greek army to the core. The RHN, having been involved very slightly, was less affected. Yet the *Averof* became caught up in several years of unseemly political coups and counter-coups sadly reminiscent of the mutiny that had infected the crew at Portsmouth in 1911. The ship's Vickers guns now fell silent, to be replaced by the strident shouts of squabbling naval commanders.

On 15 September 1922 Colonel Nikolaos Plastiras, one of the last officers to leave the Asia Minor front, stormed back across the Aegean into Athens, which he entered riding a black horse at the head of 12,000 men, overthrowing the weak civilian government and ruling by decree. His junta included the commander of the Royal Hellenic Navy, Admiral Alexander Hadjikyriakos, a grey-bearded sea-dog who personified the liberal anti-monarchist tendencies prevalent in the navy. Five politicians and the commander-in-chief of the army in Asia Minor, Lieutenant General George Hadjianestis, were tried for incompetence, found guilty and sent before a firing squad.[2] The executions shocked the Greek nation and raised a storm of international protest. King Constantine was sent packing as one of those supposedly responsible for losing the war, a move that outraged Europe's royalty. Greek public opinion simmered after the Treaty of Lausanne in July 1923 permanently handed eastern Thrace to Turkey. Constantinople, back in Turkish hands, was officially renamed Istanbul. The dream of a revived Byzantium was burst for good.

Plastiras headed what was known as the Revolutionary Committee, which included Admiral Hadjikyriakos among its members. If the Committee had limited itself purely to reforming the state structure, rooting out corruption and restoring military power and prestige, it might have done some good. Instead, it allowed itself to become entangled in partisan politics. Officers faced off into royalists and republicans, with one faction constantly intriguing against the other. Hadjikyriakos brought most of the RHN's weight on the side of the republicans, though that service, too, was plagued by divided loyalties. When an army faction rebelled against the Committee in 1923 Hadjikyriakos sent warships to bombard the insurrectionists' position on a height overlooking Corinth. The admiral was also influential in pressuring King George II, Constantine's successor, to quit the country in his father's footsteps on 19 December, and setting up the venerated Koundouriotis as regent in the king's absence. Public sympathy for the hero of Cape Helles and Limnos had surged even higher after an attempt on his life in 1921, when a bullet had penetrated his stomach.

But for all his huge national prestige, Admiral Koundouriotis was little more than a puppet in the hands of the military extremists. He was now pushing 70 and for all his exalted past, his best years were behind him. Hadjikyriakos was now boss of the Greek navy, and in 1924 he successfully intrigued with the army chiefs to abolish the monarchy through a transparently rigged plebiscite and institute a republic with Koundouriotis as president. Much as the army tried to control politics behind the façade of civilian government, corruption and incompetence were as widespread as ever. The Committee claimed to run on liberal principles, but in practice it was a thinly-concealed dictatorship, relying on so-called 'Republican Battalions' to enforce its will. Any mention of a member of the royal family, living or deceased, was made into a punishable crime.

One of the rewards that Hadjikyriakos received for membership in the Revolutionary Committee was the post of navy minister, and here RHNS *Averof* came to finish his questionable career. One of the members of Hadjikyriakos' naval clique was Commander Andreas Kolialexis, who as a reward for his support was promoted to captain and given command of the *Averof.* Not much is known about Kolialexis, but he seems to have been an unpopular man, and his appointment triggered the mass resignation of seventy-five naval officers in protest. Moreover, Kolialexis was promoted over more capable officers higher on the seniority ladder. The protesting officers demanded that Hadjikyriakos be sacked. During a stormy session of the parliament the minister said he wanted a capable man at the helm of the *Averof* to keep up prestige in view of an impending visit to Piraeus by Royal Navy ships. Few believed that sophistry, and the naval unrest spread. By July 1924 no fewer than 158 naval officers had handed in their resignations – more than half of the entire RHN officer corps. The *Averof* itself languished at the Salamis Naval Station, kept immobile by organizational chaos.

The unrest toppled the weak civilian government, and Hadjikyriakos was replaced as navy minister by the new prime minister, Themistokles Sophoulis, who was worried enough by the navy revolt to want to tackle it directly. Many dissident officers, encouraged by the change of government, took back their commissions and donned their uniforms again. But as long as Kolialexis remained captain of the *Averof,* there was bound to be trouble. Kolialexis himself, and a handful of officers in his entourage, opposed the return of the dissident officers, and to prevent them from taking up their posts again he got the *Averof* up to steam and led it out of Salamis to the offshore island of Poros, taking the rest of the cruiser fleet with it. So as not to burn his bridges with the government completely, Kolialexis offered to take Sophoulis on board the *Averof* and ferry him to his birthplace of Samos to mark a national holiday. Sophoulis agreed, but the *Averof* didn't come to pick him up at Piraeus; the prime minister instead had to reach Poros on a lowly gunboat.

The voyage back from Samos was fraught with tension. In the wardroom of the *Averof* Kolialexis begged the prime minister not to allow the dissident officers back into the navy, but Sophoulis refused to consider it. The most he would concede was to agree to send some of the officers before a court-martial before reinstating them. In the end, only minor sentences were imposed and the dissident officers returned to the navy. Kolialexis fumed in his quarters on board the *Averof.* How dare a civilian prime minister defy a member of the Revolutionary Committee? On 21 August the *Averof*'s transmitter crackled with a menacing message demanding that Sophoulis toe the Committee line. The prime minister replied with hardball of his own, ordering the removal of Kolialexis and his second-in-command from the *Averof,* but he revoked the order after a delegation of officers from the armoured cruiser called at the navy ministry to urge moderation.

Kolialexis was not mollified. His next step was to call on President Koundouriotis to step down, as the president's son Theodore Koundouriotis had been one of the naval dissidents. To back up his demands he conspicuously turned the *Averof*'s guns in the direction of downtown Athens as well as those of other ships at Salamis. He was able to take such a bellicose stance because the Revolutionary Committee and most of the army was backing him up. A posse of senior army officers had gone on board the ship to give their blessings. Kolialexis himself gave interviews to sympathetic journalists.

Sophoulis so far had been willing to reach some sort of compromise with the fractious skipper of the *Averof*. But when the ship's cannon began turning against government buildings, he took off the kid gloves. He sent demobilization orders to all the reservists serving on the mutinous ships, thus in one blow depriving the vessels of a great portion of their crews; the ships couldn't move, even if their commanders wanted. That broke the back of the budding mutiny. Kolialexis had no choice but to back down; on 23 August the fleet command was handed over temporarily to the Salamis Naval Station and Kolialexis was sentenced to two months in jail. It was an exceptionally mild penalty in the circumstances, attributable to Sophoulis' desire to mend fences where he could. Yet many in the military saw the conciliation as a sign of weakness, and hatched further plots. For the *Averof*, being reduced to a hotbed of intrigue barely a decade after it won a war was a sad come-down indeed.

Koundouriotis was beginning to tire of the political witches' cauldron which, as president, he was called on to preside over. Facing Turkish guns in the Aegean was a cinch compared to the intrigues he had to suffer from the politicians. He must have been saddened by the state of anarchy into which the Hellenic Navy (temporarily stripped of the prefix Royal) had sunk. From his mansion he watched helplessly as military factions attempted coups, first a short-lived one in November 1925 and then a more effective one under Major General Theodore Pangalos, a noted radical, in June 1925. This was the signal for Hadjikyriakos to emerge from retirement and, with the obedient Kolialexis in tow, seize the *Averof* and other ships at Salamis to back up Pangalos' seizure of power. The aging Koundouriotis had no choice but to legitimize the arrangement, but soon afterwards, when it became apparent that Pangalos was a full-time military dictator, he resigned the presidency to retire to his ancestral home on Hydra.

To Sakellariou, trying to keep up a serious naval career, these were disappointing times. 'Unimaginable hatred separated the two partisan factions [royalists and liberals], and the hostility between them reached true paroxysms,' he wrote. Pangalos made himself president in Koundouriotis' place, but his sojourn at the top was brief. His dictatorial rule, propped up by the bayonets of the Republican Battalions, proved unpopular with the rest of the military, and in August 1926 he was toppled in his turn by another officer, General George Kondylis. Pangalos was holidaying on the island of Spetses at the time, and when he heard of Kondylis' coup he fled on the torpedo boat *Pergamos* to the coast of western Greece where his ally Captain Kolialexis was stationed with a naval squadron. The small craft was in some danger in the notoriously rough seas around Cape Maleas at the southern tip of the Peloponnese. Hot on its tail was the cruiser *Kilkis*, whose commander had gone over to Kondylis, plus a hydroplane that tried to bomb the fleeing ex-dictator. Pangalos at that point judged it prudent to give himself up, as Kolialexis himself was left with just three ships. He was tried and jailed for malfeasance.

One of Kondylis' very first acts was to bring the venerable Koundouriotis back from his few months' retirement and reinstate him as president. Next he suppressed the Republican Battalions, after some serious street fighting along Kifissias Avenue in Athens that cost scores of lives. As for the *Averof,* it had already taken a holiday from this scene of partisan strife.

Chapter 7

Refit and Revolt

For most of Europe, the 1920s were years of recovery after the devastation of the First World War. The victorious great powers of Britain and France became preoccupied by the need to pay back the huge amounts of money they owed to America, without which they could never have hoped to prevail. Neither country was able to do it – even by the obvious remedy of drastically cutting back on armaments. Warships, the biggest and most expensive items of military hardware, had to be radically reassessed.

The United States Navy had by now emerged as fully the equal of the Royal Navy in tonnage and firepower, and wanted the world to acknowledge that fact. The Americans were also anxious to keep their debtors solvent and not spending huge sums on more armaments now that the war was over. In the general public revulsion over the war and a desire for disarmament, the Washington Naval Conference was called together in late 1921. Attending were delegates from the United States, Great Britain, Japan, France, Italy, China, Belgium, Portugal and the Netherlands, all powers with global maritime interests. After weeks of haggling, the major naval powers agreed to keep the tonnage of capital ships – defined as battleships and battlecruisers of 10,000 tons or more, or having a gun calibre of more than eight inches – to strict limitations and build or acquire no new ones for ten years. After that period the US Navy and Royal Navy agreed to maintain a battleship and battlecruiser fleet of

525,000 tons each, Japan would be allowed to have 325,000 tons, and France and Italy 175,000 tons each. No-one except the Americans and British were quite satisfied with this arrangement; the Japanese, in fact, keenly resented their second class status and were resolved to overturn it at the first opportunity.

The Washington Treaty of 1922 had unintended consequences. In its provision that the signatory countries scrap excess capital ship tonnage over the agreed limits, it actually paved the way for those countries to renew their fleets of smaller ships – cruisers, destroyers and submarines – in step with advancing technology. A treaty that was supposed to contribute to disarmament ended up by actually clearing the way for rapid rearmament in the following decade. Also, many naval officers were convinced that the day of the dreadnought and armoured cruiser was over anyway. The only major naval battle of the First World War involving fleets of capital ships, the Battle of Jutland, had been an exercise in inconsequential frustration. Smaller vessels, untouched by the treaty, were free to undergo development.

The warship limitations did a great deal to help the Royal Navy save money and concentrate on smaller, newer vessels. The Washington Treaty, moreover, had placed less strict limitations on aircraft carriers. All the naval powers, meanwhile, dragged their feet in scrapping excess tonnage on various pretexts. Noting these difficulties, in 1927 President Calvin Coolidge wanted to extend the 1922 treaty to cruisers and destroyers, a development that was agreed three years later. The capital ship construction ban was extended until 1936. Japan, on the other hand, inaugurated a crash programme of aircraft carrier, cruiser and destroyer construction, while Britain and America mostly stuck to the treaty terms. What did all this mean for smaller navies such as that of Greece?

The *Averof* was technically unaffected by the terms of the Washington Treaty, to which Greece was not a signatory. In any case, its 9,450-ton displacement (though not the 9.5in gun calibre) fell just short of the capital ship definition. A more important question was why a secondary naval power such as Greece needed to hang on to an obsolete armoured cruiser at all. There were, in fact, sound political and strategic reasons. Greek forces had been driven from Turkey at the end of 1922, and enmity across the Aegean continued to fester. Greece had kept its Balkan War gains of the ethnically-Greek Aegean islands, which had to be administered and protected – all 1,400 of them. Moreover, Greece had made a name for itself in the past twenty years as the prime naval power in the north-eastern Mediterranean. Even for purely prestige and symbolic reasons, the *Averof* had to be kept in commission.

But it wasn't doing much moored at Salamis except going on the occasional training cruise and serving as an unwilling stage for military coups and conspiracies. Therefore in 1925, fourteen years after launching and its baptism of fire, the Greek government decided to give Uncle George a major refit and a fresh lease on life. The shipyard of choice was Forges et Chantiers at the big French navy base at Toulon. As Admiral Koundouriotis moved from the helm of the RHN to the vastly more difficult and treacherous helm of the Greek state, the *Averof* prepared for its makeover. In November 1925 the magazines were emptied and a load of coal taken on for the five-day voyage. On arrival at Toulon on 16 November, the *Averof* and French coastal batteries exchanged twenty-one-gun courtesy salutes. Fifteen more were fired as a senior French admiral boarded the ship to welcome it. Two days later the *Averof* was dry-docked.

First, all twenty-two Belleville water tube boilers were replaced. The coal-firing system was retained; installing more modern oil-fired engines would have been expensive, and moreover not justified by future expectations of the aging cruiser. Then the three useless 21in torpedo tubes, one in the stern and two on each side below the bridge, were removed. Uncle George had never had to fire a torpedo in anger (though there were a few anxious moments during the Battle of Cape Helles when a torpedo fired itself and narrowly missed the cruiser *Psara*), and couldn't be expected to do so in the future. Also taken off were some of the lighter guns, replaced by anti-aircraft guns. The electrics and heating were thoroughly overhauled, and new cranes fitted to swing the pinnaces over the side. The most visible improvement was the installation of a new and stronger tripod foremast topped by a heavily-armoured octagonal fire-control post equipped with optical range-finders, kept high to be clear of the smoke from the funnels. In December 1926, after half a year of work and a payment of £200,000 to Forges et Chantiers, the *Averof* steamed out of Toulon and resumed its honoured place at Salamis as the flagship of the RHN, doing little except just being there as a national symbol, rather like the Parthenon overlooking Athens.

One day in February 1935 the engine-room of the *Averof* witnessed an extraordinary spectacle: artificers were busy removing the cylinder cam-heads. They were acting on the direct orders of ex-Admiral Hadjikyriakos, now back in the navy minister's chair after a period of turbulent liberal rule and determined to thwart yet another hatching coup d'etat. Seven years before, the 73-year-old Koundouriotis had finally resigned the presidency, sickened by the intrigues of the politicians, and gone to stay in dignified and now-permanent retirement at his home overlooking the sea on Hydra. He was hardly missed. A new coup by leading liberals in the military was in the final stages of planning; King George II was preparing to return to Greece, and the liberals wanted to prevent him at all costs. Part of the plot was to lead the *Averof* and the rest of the fleet up to northern Greek waters as a show of force to back the coup, whose main intention was to keep the king away. Kolialexis, now a commodore, was a prime mover in the plot. Even the venerable Venizelos so far forgot his statesmanlike instincts by lending his name to the coup, which broke out on 1 March.

But the plotters hadn't counted on Hadjikyriakos, who had no intention of letting the fleet be used in that way; in fact, he had switched his allegiance to the government and king and had assigned a 136-man guard to the Salamis naval station and appointed pro-government officers to command the ships. Without cylinder cam-heads, the *Averof* was immobilized. Hadjikyriakos had also halted supplies of fuel and munitions. Nonetheless, the navy plotters under Rear Admiral Ioannis Demestichas, the fleet commander, got together with Kolialexis and thirty liberal officers to stage a commando-type raid on the Salamis base. The guard at Perama, on the mainland opposite Salamis, was overpowered and the telephone lines cut. While Kolialexis' team occupied the naval station headquarters, Demestichas sailed up to the *Averof* in a motor launch and had little trouble taking control of the ship thanks to a fifth column inside. The missing cylinder heads were soon found and replaced.

A similar fate overtook the submarines *Katsonis* and *Nereus*, though the crews of the destroyers *Panthir* and *Ierax* were made of tougher stuff and put up a stout resistance. But within a matter of hours the anti-royal coup prevailed and by nightfall the whole fleet was in insurrectionist hands. At 3.00 am on 2 March the *Averof* and the rest of the fleet slid out of Salamis to sail north. The initial destinations were the ports of Thessaloniki and Kavala, where they would use their guns to back up the Third and Fourth Corps of the Greek army which were in the forefront of the insurrection. But Demestichas changed his mind; he wanted to sail south to Crete, where his political master Venizelos was waiting. On the way south the *Averof*'s radio crackled around the clock with orders to military units around Greece to join the coup. Rough weather on the journey, however, all but immobilized the submarine *Katsonis*, which had to abort the voyage. Also, the Royal Hellenic Air Force, loyal to the government, sent aircraft to shadow the ships and relay regular reports back to Athens. The *Averof* made it safely to Souda Bay in Crete on the evening of 2 March, but Venizelos wasn't too happy to see it there; he would have preferred the fleet to keep to its original plan to sail north, where there were more chances of the coup's success.

The government in Athens reacted swiftly. Military units in the Peloponnese loyal to Athens were placed on the alert. A decision was made to borrow bomber aircraft from Yugoslavia to send against the *Averof* – so far had partisan bitterness erased the memory of the ship's contribution to Greek history two decades before. Fortunately, before that could come about, Hadjikyriakos was sacked for failing to prevent the takeover of the fleet and replaced as navy minister by Sophocles Dousmanis, the *Averof*'s ex-captain who had fought the battles of Cape Helles and Limnos under Koundouriotis. Dousmanis mobilized those ships that had remained loyal to the government, such as the destroyers *Panthir* and *Ierax*, while the approaches to Thessaloniki were sown with mines and the shore batteries alerted. Loyal naval personnel at Salamis, meanwhile, hurriedly readied three of the remaining destroyers as well as a handful of submarines, to send in pursuit of the insurrectionist fleet. Commanding this force was none other than Alexander Sakellariou, now a rear admiral and a confirmed conservative royalist.

News of the unrest by now had spread beyond Greece's borders, with the result that on 7 March one British and two French warships sailed into Phaleron Bay south of Athens, ostensibly to protect British and French citizens but in actuality to back up the Athens government and ensure the return of King George. Britain in particular was eager to do anything towards bringing back the Greek royal family. In the north, insurrectionist commanders delayed and dithered, allowing the government to mass loyal forces east of Thessaloniki. The *Averof* duly sailed into Kavala, there to receive orders to move with the other ships to Lesvos in the Aegean. In a telling demonstration of the dictum that history repeats itself as farce, the *Averof* led the forces that took over Lesvos, Chios and Samos, this time not from any foreign enemy but from fellow-Greeks!

The insurrectionists' success was short-lived. Incompetent command in the north allowed government forces to get the upper hand within a few days. At sea, the *Averof* and other ships faced a critical fuel shortage, made no better by an urgent and futile request by the defeated rebels to be evacuated from Kavala. Sakellariou's loyalist flotilla steamed into the port at 7.00 am on 10 March and promptly opened fire on the light cruiser *Elli* docked along the sea-break. The firing was far from accurate: more shells fell in the town than on the ship, killing several people. The *Elli* escaped with minor superstructure damage and in fact, fired back with eleven rounds which didn't hit anything. At 8.30 pm Sakellariou withdrew under fire from insurrectionist field guns.

But the rebels' bolt had been shot. Venizelos had made a grave miscalculation, in fact the gravest of an otherwise brilliant political career that had now come to an inglorious end. As the government forces prevailed, there was nothing for him now to do except flee the country. The *Averof* played its last part in the sorry act imposed upon it by sailing to Crete to pick him up and ferrying him to the island of Kasos. From there he boarded an Italian boat to Italian-occupied Rhodes and sailed off to exile in Italy. The submarine *Katsonis* dived and ended up at Leros, where the Italian authorities impounded it for return to its rightful owners. By 12 March the loyal RHN had restored order through the Aegean islands.

Shortly afterwards the *Averof* left Greek waters to repeat its first assignment of 1911 – to represent the RHN at the 1935 Spithead naval review to mark the silver jubilee of King George V. Sixth in the line of foreign warships steaming off the point, the *Averof* was clearly one of the eldest, its quaint concave pre-dreadnought prow contrasting with the pointy bows of the newer vessels. In fact, it was the only foreign ship present to have taken part in both the 1911 and 1935 reviews. Other memories of past glories were revived briefly in 1937, when the *Averof* sailed to Istanbul in return for a visit to Greece the previous year of the Turkish battlecruiser *Yavuz*, which was none other than the ex-*Goeben* of the First World War notoriety. Relations between Greece and Turkey had improved vastly since the thunderous days of the Balkan and Asia Minor wars, and as a second major conflict loomed over the continent of Europe, the two countries were close to being allies. The *Averof* moored off the imposing Dolma Bahce palace, the home of President Atatürk (ex-General Mustafa Kemal), and for a few days it was old Constantinople all over again, as Uncle George's decks echoed to the clink of champagne glasses in a series of glittering cocktail parties. Well might the crew enjoy the moment of high living, as grimmer days were about to overrun the *Averof.*

The attempted coup of 1935 had strong repercussions. Loyalists howled for the ringleaders to be shot; an intimidated court-martial sentenced to death sixty officers, fifty-five of whom had already fled abroad. Remarkably, the two naval officers among the accused received pardons. In the end, two lieutenant generals and one major had to face the firing squad. Some 2,000 liberal officers were cashiered from all three services, with the purge extending to the police and judiciary. As a semblance of normality appeared to be returning to political life, the way was clear now for King George II to be recalled to his throne as a symbol of hoped-for stability. The military, now firmly in royalist hands, pressed for such a solution. On 3 November a national plebiscite brought back the king. The proportion in favour was 97 percent, lending weight to the charge that the vote was rigged, even though public opinion had swung heavily in favour of George. Yet political agitation on the left continued, until in the spring of 1936 a royalist prime minister and former general, Ioannis Metaxas, got the political establishment to grant him extraordinary powers, which he hardened into an outright dictatorship on the Mussolinian model in August of that year. But by now the shadows of war were gathering over Europe and Greece needed a strong hand at the helm.

Chapter 8

To Fight Another Day

S hort and stout and short-sighted, Metaxas was an unprepossessing man to look at. But he had probably the keenest intellect of any other Greek leader of the twentieth century, and an iron sense of purpose to match. While a young officer he had been sent to Kaiser Wilhelm's top staff college, the *Kriegsakademie* in Berlin, where his brilliant record earned the admiration of his German professors. One of his priorities on assuming power was Greece's rearmament. One day he boarded the *Averof* to observe naval manoeuvres. To a crewmember, 'what [Metaxas] lacked in stature he made up for in brains.'

At the end of 1939 disturbing messages began reaching Rear Admiral Sakellariou, now the chief of the Naval Staff with direct access to both Metaxas and the king. For several months Italian warships had been visiting Greek ports, and their crews in the bars and cafes had been singing a song that grated on the Greeks' sensibilities:

Sbarcheremo al Pireo e conquisteremo tutto l'Egeo!

'We'll disembark at Piraeus and conquer the whole Aegean!' The expansionist plans of Mussolini's Italy were the most open of secrets, but the Greek government so far had shrugged them off, confident in an unwritten pledge of support from Britain, whose Royal Navy maintained a powerful presence in the Mediterranean. But other things bothered Sakellariou, such as the constant harassment of Greek warships at sea by Italian ships and planes. Such incidents escalated after Italy entered the European war in 1940. On 12 July Italian bombers attacked the RHN supply ship *Orion* supplying a lighthouse off Crete. Four days later the RHN submarine base at Navpaktos in the Gulf of Corinth was bombed, with a repeat attack at the end of July. On 2 August Italian aircraft attacked the Greek contraband-chaser *A6* between Salamis and Aigina, practically within sight of Athens. Miraculously, there were no casualties.

The crisis took a quantum leap on 15 August when an Italian submarine torpedoed the light cruiser *Elli* docked at the island of Tinos for a religious festival. This was the same *Elli* that had come under Greek loyalist fire at Kavala just five years before. This time several crewmembers were killed. Hearing of the incident, Sakellariou had the Italian naval attaché called in for an explanation. The attaché lamely claimed the attack could not have come from an Italian vessel, but fragments of torpedoes that had missed the *Elli* and hit the jetty were scattered around, and Sakellariou ordered them collected. Their markings proved their Italian manufacture. From that date everyone in Greece, from Metaxas and the king on down, knew that the country was on a collision course with Italy. But no-one knew when the impact would come.

Metaxas telephoned Sakellariou at 11.00 pm on 27 October. 'Sleep easy tonight,' the prime minister told the admiral. For several days all the chiefs of staff had been on alert. But a good night's sleep was what neither man would get, as four hours later Metaxas was awakened by the Italian ambassador who had driven up with Mussolini's demand for Italian units to enter Greece. Metaxas flatly refused, and Greece was in the war. Sakellariou was awakened at 3.00 am on 28 October by Metaxas' orders: 'Get downtown and issue any naval mobilization orders you have. Set your staff plans in motion for war. God help us and the Virgin Mary be with us.' Leaving his family in bed, the admiral drove to navy headquarters. A clear Athenian dawn was breaking but his mind was in turmoil.

> I felt the whole weight of the great responsibility fall on my shoulders [he wrote later]. Would my forecasts prove correct? All those years of work, plans and studies – were they based on proper calculations? Would luck, that inseparable part of any military success, be with us?

Ioannis Haniotis, a young reservist seaman, had just got out of bed at his home in Athens when a neighbour girl arrived and told him the country was at war. As the streets echoed to the peal of church bells, Haniotis switched on the radio to hear that he was being called back to the navy. By lunchtime, in his new dark blue uniform with the red insignia of a leading seaman, he was nervously tucking into pasta on the *Averof.*

As the Italian divisions poured over the Albanian border into Greece, and the Greek army gathered its scattered units for a fanatic resistance, Sakellariou assessed his own units. These were the *Averof,* by now obsolete and quite unfit for combat at sea; ten destroyers and six submarines, plus an assortment of torpedo boats and auxiliary craft. On 1 November a formation of Italian bombers appeared over Salamis at a great height. As the alarm sounded, the *Averof*'s crew raced for cover while the anti-aircraft guns opened up – the first time the four new Vickers 76mm and six Rheinmetall 37mm guns belched in anger. All the enemy bombs went wide, except for one that hit the old decommissioned cruiser *Limnos,* damaging it but not sinking it. This raid moved Sakellariou to order the *Averof* to sail west through the Salamis channel to a more secure mooring in

Eleusis Bay, where it was to remain for the next seven months until the German invasion of Greece.

In the years before the war the army had received most of the benefits of rearmament, with relatively little going to the navy and even less to the RHAF. The remaining cruisers of the Balkan War era had all gone, the *Limnos* and the torpedoed *Elli* being the last. However, the British naval attaché in Athens, Rear Admiral Charles Turle, was the RHN's main liaison with the Royal Navy Mediterranean Fleet under Admiral Sir Andrew Cunningham, and so as long as support was assured from that sector, Sakellariou could plan with a cool head.

The RHN's main wartime task was to escort troopships from Crete and the islands to the mainland where the soldiers could be sent on to the front. That this was accomplished over a period of six months without the loss of a single troopship or soldier to the Italian submarines and aircraft prowling the Aegean says a great deal for the professionalism of the Greek navy under Sakellariou. The RHAF's three naval cooperation squadrons, some equipped with modern Avro Anson maritime patrol aircraft, also performed sterling service under difficult weather conditions.

The entire third-year class of the naval academy had been prematurely graduated with non-commissioned warrant officer rank and assigned *en masse* to the *Averof*, where Captain Michail Zarokostas tried to find them things to do. As the RHN's destroyers and submarines were sent on hazardous missions in the Ionian Sea, the immobile personnel on board the immobile *Averof* were left chafing at the bit. Those with connections wangled temporary transfers to destroyers. The others would have to wait for their moment. One midshipman was kept busy ensuring that the nightly blackout was complete, puttering in a boat around the hull to see that not a chink of light came out of the portholes. Those months of inactivity before the German invasion could have had something to do with the crew frustration that erupted in the near-mutiny of April 1941.

> The old ship remained tied up at Eleusis and took no part in operations [Leading Seaman Haniotis wrote later]. We rejoiced at the Greek victories on the Albanian front and at our Navy's actions. Those were unforgettable months!

Seamen would gather around the radios and eagerly follow the breathless communiqués as the Greek army captured town after town in Albania. All were fans of Greece's greatest pop singer, Sophia Vembo, whose sultry voice dominated the airwaves with stinging satires about Mussolini and the Italians.

Yet the Greek-Italian conflict was inevitably an army show above all, and of course the boys in khaki reaped almost all the glory, especially after the Italians were halted in the Battle of Kalpaki and driven back across the Albanian border, and the Greeks, their bayonets red with enemy blood, charged after them in the snow. Church bells rang joyously every week with some new triumph of Greek arms. The navy's task, by contrast, was as unglamorous as it was necessary. It was the universal plaint of the naval officer in the twentieth century that the navy had to struggle for exposure in the news media, which tend to favour first the air force and then the army for role models of glamour. Few ordinary people stopped to realize, for example, that Germany's defeat in the First World War had been the result just as much of the Royal Navy's blockade of German ports as of the struggle in the trenches. Or that many Greek soldiers were able to reach the Albanian front because the navy had enabled them to get there in the first place.

Sakellariou brought up the subject with Metaxas and King George. He felt his fleet could get a piece of the action by running interference with Italian supply ships plying the route between the heel of Italy and Albanian ports across the Otranto strait. Metaxas agreed, and allowed RHN destroyers to enter the Adriatic Sea. Two of them shelled Italian positions in northwest Greece. The submarines, meanwhile, carried out aggressive patrols in the same sector, scoring a few hits on enemy troopships at great risk to themselves.

As for the *Averof*, no-one quite knew what to do with it. It was far too old for any kind of meaningful active service, but at the same time too much of a national icon to send to the breakers' yard. Hulking Uncle George was the biggest and most imposing warship the Greeks had ever had. Yet, moored as it was in Eleusis Bay, it was a sitting duck for enemy bombers. By sheer luck, no Italian bomb had yet hit it, but that of course was no guarantee of its safety. The problem became more acute in early 1941 as it became dismayingly obvious that Hitler would pull the Duce's chestnuts out of the fire by invading Greece. On 29 January Metaxas, whose firm hand at Greece's helm had enabled the country to repel the first Axis assault, died unexpectedly, leaving the country leaderless.

The blow fell on 6 April as German columns smashed through the Greek and British defences in northern Greece while the Luftwaffe bombed and strafed anything that moved. Within a matter of days the Germans were at the gates of Athens, with some 55,000 Greek and Allied troops racing for the exits in a chaotic and costly Mediterranean Dunkirk. The Royal Navy cruisers HMS *Calcutta* and *Coventry*, crammed with demoralized troops, ran the gauntlet to Crete, later to be joined by HMS *Orion*, *Perth* and *Phoebus*.

When the Germans attacked, the *Averof* was serving as the headquarters of the fleet commander, Rear Admiral Epaminondas Kavvadias. Droves of Luftwaffe planes roared over the ship, dropping bombs that raised great geysers on either side and drenched the superstructure in seawater but somehow failed to hit the ship itself. To Haniotis, those were 'nightmare' hours. 'The *Averof* must have had a guardian angel,' said Able Seaman Panayotis Gorgas, who had served on the ship since the beginning of the war, echoing a near-universal belief. The ship's powerful anti-aircraft guns had put the enemy raiders off their aim, but manning them was an ordeal. Anti-aircraft gun duty quickly became known as the 'death shift,' though no-one was killed. One crewmember watched as a Stuka screamed down, strafing the stern at low height; the plane failed to recover height and smacked into the hillside overlooking the bay, possibly hit by the ship's fire. Most of the German bombing, however, was aimed at the commercial port of Piraeus and its approaches. The submarine force was recuperating at Salamis after its heroic efforts in the Adriatic, though a couple of destroyers were sunk in the bays southwest of Athens. In the confusion in Athens, Sakellariou had been appointed vice-premier and navy minister. He had available, besides the *Averof,* ten destroyers, five submarines, nine auxiliary ships, thirteen torpedo boats and nine requisitioned civilian vessels. The slow *Averof* was a cause of especial concern, as Sakellariou doubted whether it could make the mad dash first to Crete and then to Alexandria without being caught. If not, he was prepared to have it sunk himself, but decided to ask the British Admiralty first.

As the German columns drove relentlessly south, in the evening of 17 April the *Averof*'s second-in-command, Commander Papavasiliou, assembled the officers in Koundouriotis' wood-panelled admiral's quarters in the stern. 'The Germans are at Thebes,' Papavasiliou said, 'and tomorrow their tanks will be within sight. For us the war is over. The *Averof* is an old ship and can't keep up with the rest of the fleet.' There were some protests from the assembled officers, as they believed they knew where Papavasiliou was going with this –

the words were a preamble to an announcement that Uncle George would have to be scuttled. The s-word seems not to have actually been uttered, as after some minutes of argument, the commander said he was going ashore to consult with Sakellariou in the navy ministry.

It was now about 8.00 pm and darkness had fallen. The most senior officer present, Lieutenant Commander Panayotis Damilatis, the chief gunnery officer, spoke up. 'Sir, we'll wait for you until eleven o'clock.' The unspoken corollary was unmistakable: if Papavasiliou wasn't back by then, Damilatis would assume provisional command of the ship, and sail. Papavasiliou then said that anyone who wanted to go home could get off the ship with him. There was a general rush for the motor launch that alarmed even those men who elected to stay on. Warrant Officer (later Commodore) Constantine Moschos, one of the third-year naval cadets rushed into service, had to fire a few shots into the air to get the launch to move off before it could become overloaded. To be fair, almost all the older crew and married men who felt they could not abandon their families to an unknown fate chose to go. Gorgas saw them getting into boats and prepared to follow them, but the thought occurred to him that as his 'home' in central Greece had by now been overrun by the Germans, an uncertain future on the *Averof* was better than living under the German heel. Most of the younger single men, with few or no family obligations and infected by an urge for adventure, similarly elected to stay with the ship, come what may. The ship's chaplain, Father Dimitrios Papanikolopoulos, stood firm with those who wanted to sail, 'even with just ten men if necessary.' Uncle George was coaled up and ready to move to Crete with some 300 crew on board. Some were reminded of the Athenian leader Themistokles, whose 'wooden walls' – i.e. the Athenian navy – had saved Greece at that very spot in 480 BC. The general feeling was well summed up by Haniotis:

Personally, like all of us, I grieved to leave my country. But no way could I stay when the Germans were there. I wanted to fight. I followed my ship, my captain, my officers and petty officers, my mates.

Not many, if any, of the men who remained on board were aware that a decision had in fact been made to scuttle the ship. Time bombs had been secretly planted under the powder magazines for the purpose. The Rheinmetall guns had been dismantled and sent ashore, a development which, to Haniotis, 'made us feel very bad, as if we were being abandoned to our fate'. Actually, the guns were reinstalled a few days later. Chief Petty Officer Dimos Doxiadis had just reported for duty on board the ship, transferred from shore duties, on 17 April in the middle of the confusion. As he'd already made up his mind to continue fighting, he was one of the men who remained on board after the unwilling had departed. In company with the similarly-vulnerable torpedo boats, the *Averof* was to make the hazardous passage to Souda Bay at a moment's notice. The time came that same night, when the Royal Navy sloop HMS *Salvia* finished clearing the mines that the Luftwaffe had recently sown off the entrance to the Salamis channel. Papavasiliou had returned on time with a fresh order to abandon the vessel, but he was driven off with hoots and catcalls. Lieutenant Commander Damilatis, meanwhile, had gone ahead and assumed provisional command in the absence ashore of the *Averof*'s new commander, Captain Ioannis Vlachopoulos, and was all for escaping and joining the wider fight. As the ship nosed quietly out of the channel it came up against the lowered boom at the channel mouth. The boom guardhouse said it had orders not to let the ship leave and sent a message to Sakellariou, who replied, 'in the name of the endangered country,' with an order for the ship to remain where it was.

Damilatis promptly radioed back: 'Officers and men of the *Averof* request the chief of staff to board ship to continue the fight.'[1] If the venerable *Averof* was fated to end its days, what better way than to go down fighting?

Sakellariou (though he tried to cover up the uncomfortable fact in his memoirs) was determined to scuttle the cruiser, and repeated his order more peremptorily, warning that otherwise 'friendly as well as enemy aircraft' would sink the ship. The bridge personnel looked at one another in confusion. Why 'friendly?' While that exchange was in progress, Gorgas and some of the crew lowered themselves in a boat, and armed with sledgehammers, wire-cutters and hacksaws, cut the thick cables securing the boom. Its way now free, the armoured cruiser slipped through, with Gorgas and the others in the boat behind rowing frantically to catch up. Even the guardhouse flashed a good luck signal. Sakellariou, accepting the inevitable, sent a final despairing message: 'Wait for your commander.' Captain Vlachopoulos had been left behind in the haste, but Damilatis was quite prepared to do without him if necessary. Vlachopoulos eventually caught up on a motor launch and promptly ordered the ship to be turned around. Damilatis retorted that the crew would not tolerate retreat. As Doxiadis witnessed the scene, Vlachopoulos thought for a moment, and muttered, 'I suppose you're right.' (For that moment of courage and common sense, Vlachopoulos was later awarded the Military Cross Third Class.) A beaten Sakellariou had no choice but to message him: 'God be with you.' The threat of 'friendly' fire, as most suspected, turned out to be empty.

The following daybreak found the ship moving slowly, hugging the east coast of the Peloponnese so the telltale smoke trail would not be seen against the dark mountains to starboard. This was Vlachopoulos' idea, according to Chief Petty Officer Constantine Skiadopoulos:

We were lucky to have Vlachopoulos, otherwise we would have been sunk by German air attack [Skiadopoulos wrote later]. This was because he decided not to sail straight for Crete through the open sea but to hug the east coast of the Peloponnese ... When night fell we increased speed and turned east.

All the way down, the crew kept an anxious lookout for Stukas, but none appeared. The second night was Orthodox Good Friday, and the blacked-out deck of the *Averof* presented an eerie sight as the crew attended the solemn Crucifixion service without lighting a single candle. The next morning the ship arrived at Souda Bay, anchoring alongside the half-sunken hulk of the Royal Navy cruiser HMS *York*, destroyed by Italian manned torpedoes a month before. The sun was not yet fully up when Italian bombers attacked the bay; not only did the *Averof*'s redoubtable defences bring one of the raiders down, but yet again the cruiser escaped unscathed. Gorgas, for one, needed no more convincing that Uncle George enjoyed some sort of divine protection. Only a few dozen dinner plates were broken.

The destination of the destroyers and submarines had not yet been decided. All ammunition and stores were to be sent on to Souda Bay, while all nonessential naval personnel were sent on indefinite leave – to all intents and purposes demobilized. Sakellariou also had to deal with serious demoralization and defeatism in the navy ranks. Before the *Averof* sailed for Crete, its crew had been infected as badly as the rest, with the result that Kavvadias removed his headquarters to shore. The crew of the destroyer *Aetos* mutinied after witnessing well-connected Greeks fleeing on board with their money and poodles, not to carry on the fight but merely to escape the discomforts of enemy occupation!

Whatever the motives for the unrest, Sakellariou had to play hardball. He had the commanders of the destroyers *Aetos* and

Spetsai arrested for cowardice and issued the following order: 'Everyone is hereby notified that anyone who does not obey orders unquestioningly will be shot on the spot. I will personally bear responsibility for each execution.' To drive the point home, he sent before the firing squad one officer who not only had deserted his destroyer but also had absconded with the seamen's pay. The situation in the submarine squadron was no better, as a majority of the commanders refused to sail them to Egypt. They changed their minds when the Luftwaffe bombed the destroyers *King George* and *Queen Olga*, damaging the former beyond repair.

Sakellariou had got Turle to approve the *Averof*'s inclusion in Allied Convoy AS26 bound for Alexandria. Events rushed one upon the other. The Germans were at the gates of Athens. The day after the *Averof* made its escape, Metaxas' successor as prime minister, a mild ex-banker, broke under the strain and put a bullet in his head. King George and his government prepared to flee to Crete. The RHN, despite the severest measures, remained in the throes of defeatism and mutiny. Greece officially capitulated on 20 April. Everyone now expected the Germans to launch a massive attack on Crete. Vlachopoulos realized that his historic cruiser was far too vulnerable at Souda Bay, so on 21 April he joined up with HMS *Carlisle*, a light cruiser, in Convoy AS26 bound for Alexandria. The mood on board was sombre.

> We were leaving our country as it was being enslaved [Gorgas remembered later]. We thought of our families and loved ones – would we ever see them again? Would my parents survive? I hadn't even got to say goodbye to them. How would they know if I was alive or dead? Those were my thoughts as Crete disappeared behind us.

Doxiadis, for his part, was young enough to enjoy the sense of adventure. But the two–day, 500-mile trip was fraught with hazard. Luftwaffe Junkers Ju88 attack bombers repeatedly hurtled out of the sky at the ships, but for the umpteenth time Uncle George, ploughing stolidly through the unfamiliar waters of the southern Mediterranean, sometimes firing back, escaped harm and sailed unscratched into Alexandria on 23 April. Even in Alexandria the ship wasn't safe. Whenever enemy aircraft came over Uncle George would open up with his guns and help see them off. He'd never lost a battle, and wasn't about to do so now.

Rear Admiral Sakellariou, meanwhile, had his hands full. Many on board the *Averof* had wondered at his intransigent attitude in insisting that the ship on which he himself had served with great pride be scuttled. According to Doxiadis' account, the crusty chief of staff had been under the impression that the crew had mutinied and that Damilatis was merely a puppet of a musician petty officer believed to be in control. Hence his tough stand, for which he eventually apologized in Alexandria. After the *Averof*'s departure Sakellariou centred his concern on the remaining destroyers in the fleet. The newest one, the *Queen Olga*, came under air attack on 20 April; a midshipman on the bridge was killed. Two days later the ship was deputed to carry fleeing government members and their families to Crete. While the *Koundouriotis* joined the *Averof* in Convoy AS26 and made it to Egypt, some sixty Stukas howled out of the sky onto the destroyer *Hydra* after it set out from Piraeus. The ship was able to zigzag out of the way of the first wave of bombs, but the second wave fell alongside the ship, shattering the hull and killing most of the men above decks. Gunners bravely continued to pour fire into the attacking aircraft while the destroyer lost speed. The surviving crewmembers were ordered to abandon ship, and shortly afterwards the *Hydra* sank, taking with it its captain who, though grievously wounded, refused to leave the vessel, and his second-in-command.

The *Spetsai* had the vital task of removing Greece's gold reserves to safety in Egypt. It, too, came under air attack but reached its destination without damage. German bombers caught the destroyer *Psara* in Megara Bay, sinking it with two large bombs through the foredeck. Before it slid beneath the waves, a gunner claimed to have brought down a Stuka. Also making it to Alexandria after running the Cretan gauntlet were the *Aetos, Leon, Panthir* and *Ierax*. Then the RHN submarines began arriving: the *Papanikolis, Katsonis, Triton, Nereus* and *Glavkos*. Sakellariou had personally seen them off at Salamis. 'Everyone was weeping with joy,' he wrote later, 'because our flag would not be dishonoured' by the vessels' surrender to the Germans.

Meanwhile King George, shocked by his prime minister's suicide, asked Sakellariou if he would accept the position of vice-premier with the king himself as acting prime minister. The admiral had a low opinion of politicians and the last thing he wanted was to become one of them. He replied that he would prefer to remain at the head of the navy, where he could be of far more use to his country. But the king brushed aside the refusal and within a few hours he found himself being sworn in as vice-premier and navy minister. It proved to be an empty honour. He was not invited to cabinet meetings, which was actually something of a relief as he could devote his undivided attention to his beleaguered warships.

Sakellariou was one of the very last ranking Greeks to abandon Athens before the Germans rolled in. The king and his new prime minister, a fawning politician named Emmanuel Tsouderos, had fled the coop to Crete on 23 April. Two days later, Major General George Heywood, the Allied commander-in-chief on Greek soil, also decided it was time to go. Sakellariou went home to say goodbye to his wife and thirteen-year-old daughter. They had wanted to go with him but he judged they would be safer where they were. As he picked up a packed suitcase, the girl began to cry and he tried to console her. 'Don't forget you're an admiral's daughter,' he said. 'As a military daughter you're not supposed to cry. You should stay here to show young Greeks that they should endure slavery with their heads high.' At 3.30 pm he joined General Heywood at the mediaeval Byzantine church at Dafni in the outer western suburbs of Athens. There were also Rear Admiral Turle and the single remaining Greek government minister. Before setting out on the road to Corinth and Nafplion, where they could expect to be evacuated, Sakellariou ducked briefly into the dark church under the glowering icon of the Almighty beneath the central dome and lit a candle. He had no way of knowing if he would ever see his country or loved ones again.

With the rapidly advancing German units hard on their heels, and the Luftwaffe roaring overhead at low height with scarcely any interruption, the party made its way to Nafplion, where they hid under olive trees to await rescue by sea. A peasant walked up to Sakellariou, thinking him to be a British officer, and offered his humble dwelling to him and Heywood and the other British officers in the party. The peasant's wife set a small table and poured glasses of rustic wine. 'Don't you worry about us,' the farmer said, raising his glass. 'Just save yourselves. Don't worry about a thing. We'll lick 'em!' The peasant's simple courage and confidence made a huge impression on Heywood, and even Sakellariou received a dose of new resolve. After another day of Luftwaffe strafing, sometimes so low that the pilots' faces could be clearly seen, a Royal Air Force Short Sunderland flying boat came to airlift them all to Crete. As the overloaded plane rose heavily over the port of Nafplion, Sakellariou saw the entire waterfront lit up by a blazing transport in the harbour.

Chapter 9

Indian Summer

S akellariou disembarked at Alexandria on 12 May to find the *Averof* and the other fourteen ships of what was left of the Royal Hellenic Navy at anchor in the port. Under the white Egyptian sunlight there was no more idyllic surrounding than the palm-fringed cosmopolitan Corniche and smart Cecil Hotel. But the war caught up soon enough; that same night an enemy raid turned the seafront into a blazing Wagnerian backdrop while the *Averof* pounded away stoutly with its anti-aircraft guns. Yet again the ship wasn't hit – by now, no surprise. Shortly afterwards, Doxiadis was promoted to acting warrant officer and given a shore job in the Greek navy ministry-in-exile.

Sakellariou had a great deal to do to reorganize the remnant of the RHN to make it into a fit partner for the Royal Navy. Thanks to helpful British base accounts officers, he was able to place the Greek navy in Egypt on a sound financial and legal footing. Yet there were persistent doubts about whether the remnant of the Greek fleet was in a condition to continue the war on the Allied side. The *Averof* was indeed making itself useful by serving as a floating naval academy where ex-cadet chief petty officers and warrant officers could continue their courses and expect to graduate to a commission. Some of them were assigned to man the anti-aircraft guns or the searchlights that picked out the German bombers droning over almost nightly. 'We were a floating gun battery,' recalled Papasifakis.

The raids would go on for hours. On one such raid a German air-sown mine was seen to be floating down right onto the *Averof*. Panic reigned until the mine plopped into the sea mere feet away from the hull, carried by a sudden wind that, according to Papasifakis, ruffled the waves at that precise moment, saving the ship one more time. The mine was defused the next day.

But such moments of dedication to duty were becoming less and less frequent. One sign of the simmering discontent was the decision to house the naval court-martial on the *Averof*. Instances of insubordination and mutiny among the RHN crews were multiplying. A few death sentences were imposed, to be commuted into detention in the infamous disciplinary camps dotting Palestine, but they seemed to have little effect. The causes of the unrest were many and varied. The lightning-quick German conquest of Greece had generally depressed morale; defeatism was still rampant, with many questioning why the Greeks should keep fighting alongside the British, who were retreating in North Africa, as German propaganda in Egypt endlessly reiterated. Life, too, was pleasant in the cafés and bars of Alexandria, where the war seemed far away. The large and prosperous Greek community in Alexandria pulled out all the stops to make the men feel at home. 'Everyone looked on us as heroes,' Doxiadis recalled. Yet many seamen were deserting to the Greek merchant navy, where the pay was much higher and the discipline much looser. The ships themselves, with the exception of the *Queen Olga*, were old and worn and had suffered damage from German attacks.

Then there was the plague of Greek pre-war politics. Older officers of all three services had never quite rid themselves of the germs of the chronic royalist-liberal dispute that had sprung a series of coups and counter-coups on the country since the early 1920s. The Metaxas dictatorship had tried to iron out this old rift and place the Greek military on a proper non-political professional footing. But with the coming of the war, Metaxas' death and the German occupation, all the old vicious enmities came back with a vengeance. The liberals now joined forces with the left and the increasingly-influential Greek Communist Party, an organ of Stalin, against the supporters of the monarchy and conservative parliamentary democracy to reduce what was left of the Greek armed forces in the Middle East to near-chaos. What was more, even within the factions there was ill-feeling between the traditional officer corps and those ex-cadets who hadn't been able to graduate because of the outbreak of war, and resented their petty officer status. In the RHN entire destroyer crews were taking over the vessels in the name of the red flag, sometimes employing terror tactics. The *Averof*, as the navy's flagship, was unfortunately the scene of much of the nastiness.

From his headquarters on board the *Averof*, Sakellariou employed some of his renowned toughness into putting some backbone into the Greek navy. Early in the war he had a fractious destroyer commander placed under arrest and physically tied with a rope, in full view of the public in the middle of Athens! But his moves to set up special punishment camps for mutinous offenders were thwarted by Tsouderos, the prime minister-in-exile, who feared alienating the communists as he wanted them to help further his own political career. Sakellariou had never had much use for politicians, but he regarded Tsouderos with cold contempt as a typical example of the self-serving kind, more interested in feathering his own political nest than carrying on his country's fight against the Axis. The weak-willed King George was not much higher in his estimation, especially when he and Tsouderos moved to London to be out of harm's way. But the leftwing revolt in the Greek military was only just beginning.

Most urgent of all was the need for ship maintenance. The Royal Navy's repair dry-docks in the Middle East were employed overtime in urgent work on British ships, with no capacity to spare for anything else. Alexandria harbour was becoming crowded with British warships with nowhere else to go. The *Averof*, conspicuously obsolete, was thought to be taking up valuable space. A reprieve came when the Royal Navy agreed that Uncle George could be of some use escorting Allied convoys in the Red Sea and Arabian Sea. Moreover, there were repair centres in India, where the battered RHN ships could receive new anti-aircraft guns and sonar.

The move east was not welcomed by everyone. Some crews had become too used to the good life in Alexandria. One of these was an unbalanced Cretan midshipman serving on the *Averof* by the name of Iliomarkakis who took the lead in sowing insubordination among the rest of the crew. This man's excuse was that the ship would be condemned to inaction in strange seas; he would have preferred to see it near home waters, ready for the hoped-for liberation of Greece in the future. The notion was, in fact, a mask for communist sentiments. He found considerable support among those ex-cadet chief petty officers whose studies in the naval academy had been interrupted by war and hence were (temporarily) denied commissioned rank. However, Iliomarkakis found few takers among the senior crew, and Admiral Sakellariou scotched the incipient mutiny in person by climbing, in full uniform and monocle, up the side of the ship to make an imposing appearance on the afterdeck.

On 1 July the *Averof*, towing the submarine *Katsonis* and in the company of the repair ship *Hephaistos* and torpedo boat *Sphendoni*, put in at Port Tewfiq (now Suez Port) after traversing the Suez Canal.[1] Under its new skipper, Constantine Kondoyannis (nicknamed Cucaracha for his habit of singing the Latin American ditty of that name and dancing little jigs to it), the *Averof* stayed at Port Tewfiq for three weeks, enduring German air attacks that – miraculously yet inevitably – left the ship unscathed but sank the British passenger transport *Georgic*, anchored nearby and full of noncombatants, with great loss of life. The *Averof*'s launches were busy for hours ferrying the dead and wounded – many of them horrifically burned – to shore. Recreation was limited. If anyone wanted to go swimming, a small sheltered area of sea was set aside as the Red Sea seethed with sharks. A few lighter moments were provided by the Greek manager of the local Barclays Bank branch and nightclub, who gave the men the run of the premises and provided comfortable beds for periods of shore leave. There was the ubiquitous Greek taverna whose owner held in reserve barrels of sweet Samos wine; a lot of the men had to be carried back on the ship on stretchers after overindulgence in that powerful stuff. The club, for its part, was also a priceless hunting ground for that perennial urgent requirement of the seaman – women.

The tropical heat was an ordeal in itself. Chief Petty Officer (later Lieutenant Commander) Ioannis Ladopoulos recalled:

> From 8 in the morning to 7 in the evening we went around in swimming trunks. On the deck we would hold the hose pipe in turn and play it over one another to recover. No-one descended to his cabin. We ate and slept on the deck. We couldn't even urinate. We would mop our sweat with towels. We just melted.

On 20 July the voyage was resumed, with the next stop Port Sudan. The fearsome Sudanese *haboob* was surging up from the African hinterland, its red-hot winds blowing great clouds of sand before it. The midsummer temperatures in the Red Sea continued to be extreme, with hellish conditions prevailing in the engine and boiler rooms, despite the tropical pith helmets and shorts provided. Even the light shorts were too much to bear. At least one crewman, the chief cook, perished from heat stroke. Water from the hoses evaporated almost as soon as it left the nozzles. Stoking could only be done in the cooler part of the night, sometimes with the ship's band playing to keep the sweating stokers' spirits up. Some of the sick had to be taken to a British military hospital in Port Sudan and cooled down with ice blocks. Luckily, most of the business in Port Sudan was in the hands of Greeks, so the men of the *Averof* could look forward to cool drinks and hotel rooms on their shore leave.

Uncle George could now only manage nine knots, and the three weeks spent at Port Sudan were well spent in vital repairs. The main one was the installation of a newer oil-firing system to speed up the coal ignition, a project which took many days of work with the help of Royal Navy engineers but gave the ship a paltry three more knots of speed. Eventually the ship reached Aden, where it was given the task of escorting a convoy across the Arabian Sea to Bombay (now Mumbai), where it arrived on 10 September after a seventy-six day voyage of some 3,300 miles.

'The Greek contribution of the *Averof* to the Allied convoys in the Indian Ocean was a welcome gift to the British,' wrote Warrant Officer Moschos. 'Even though it could do no more than twelve knots because of its old boilers, its heavy guns were insurance against German raiders.'

The crew of the cruiser HMS *Barham*, a veteran of the Battle of Cape Matapan, welcomed that of the *Averof* as soon as it arrived by inviting it to a rowing contest. The ship now had yet another new commander, Captain Spyros Matesis, who eagerly accepted the challenge and got together a beefy team of engine room personnel, all expert stokers and merchant navy veterans. The Greeks won handily.

The rudimentary naval cadets' college still operated on board the *Averof,* and one of the cadets, George Alexandris, recalled being dazzled by the sights of the Orient. Like hundreds of other young men, he had escaped ravaged Greece and found his way to Egypt.

'We were the new blood in the navy,' he wrote later, so glad to be serving his country that he 'didn't care about [the possibility of] being killed'. But once in Bombay he became aware of unrest among the regular ship's crew. There was a flap when the ship sailed on a mission without its proper provisioning, with the result that some stokers stole several chickens from the officers' refrigerator and cooked them in the ship's boilers. The first the officers knew about it was when a signalman was sent below decks to wind up the engine room clocks. He detected an aroma of roast meat wafting through the vaults, and when he went to investigate he came across a party of stokers merrily chomping on pieces of chicken, washing them down with whisky. 'Hey, signalman, want a leg?' one of them said. Himself hungry, the signaller gratefully accepted a leg of chicken and a tumbler of whisky, and then felt a cold gun barrel jammed against his temple. He turned to see an officer and half a dozen seamen who had surreptitiously followed him down. Caught *in flagrante delicto*, there wasn't much the signalman could do in the way of fast talk. 'You've just blown your promotion to leading seaman,' the officer said. (The signalman was promoted six months later, thanks to a friendly officer.)

There was a historically interesting sidelight to the *Averof*'s presence in the Indian Ocean, as it was the first Greek naval presence in the region since Alexander the Great's admiral Nearchos probed those waters in the fourth century BC. But Nearchos probably had never had to put up with long months in the Indian heat. On arrival at Bombay the *Averof* received a complement of Indian stokers who could stand the extreme conditions below decks. The *Averof*'s first missions were to escort convoys to the Strait of Hormuz and back, and then to Colombo in Sri Lanka, covering nearly 5,000 miles. The first convoy was made up of a group of oil tankers carrying that most vital ingredient of warfare. 'Our hopes that we'd meet a

German raider weren't realized,' said Moschos, who had been with the ship since the beginning of the war. The next mission began on 20 December 1941 to escort a large eastbound convoy of troopships heading for Singapore that was about to be attacked by the Japanese. By that time Pearl Harbor had occurred and the war had become truly global. The *Averof* accompanied the convoy as far as Ceylon (Sri Lanka), where the British cruiser HMS *Glasgow* took over the protection and the Greek cruiser was ordered to accompany a British troopship to Colombo.

That's where the *Averof* spent Christmas 1941. On New Year's Eve the crew sat down to a party in Colombo's Grand Oriental Hotel. The hotel band, seeing the Greek naval uniforms, broke into a popular Greek hit of the late 1930s. 'It was all we could do not to cry,' Papasifakis said. At midnight a waiter popped a bottle of champagne, when a Royal Navy midshipman sitting near Moschos began to shake uncontrollably. It turned out that the man was one of the few survivors of the battleship HMS *Prince of Wales*, sunk by the Japanese three weeks before, and the popping of the cork had triggered a panic reaction. Then some US Navy personnel present began to deride the British for needing American help to evacuate their families from Singapore, triggering a vicious Anglo-American brawl witnessed by an incredulous Moschos – who that day, 1 January, received his commission as technically having completed his naval college training. (Later that month Moschos was transferred to the destroyer *Queen Olga* which had escaped the hell of the Aegean and was docked at Calcutta, probably the nearest the RHN ever got to the Japanese.)

The trembling British officer in Colombo was the first inkling which the crewmen of the *Averof* received of the sinking of HMS *Prince of Wales* and *Repulse*. Lieutenant Constantine Tsallis, for one, was seriously shaken.

We all thought the war was lost then [Tsallis recalled]. But our
British liaison officer, [RNVR] Lieutenant Robert Swan, tried
to revive our spirits. On the way back to Bombay he would keep
telling us, 'The war is not lost just because we lost two ships.'

The *Averof*'s third Indian Ocean mission came soon afterwards, in
January 1942. At the entrance to the Persian Gulf Matesis glimpsed
a suspicious-looking vessel at a great distance. He knew that German
raiders operated in the region, often disguised as merchantmen but
hiding powerful guns. Sounding battle stations, Matesis ordered
the helmsman to steer in the mystery ship's direction, but the ship
picked up speed and vanished. Papasifakis was 'disappointed that
we didn't get to fight'. On that same trip, the crew marvelled at the
brilliance of the phosphorescent plankton in the *Averof*'s bow wave;
one night the light was so intense that it actually threw shadows on
the cabin walls.

'The ship might have had a few decades on its back, but its heavy
guns ensured that it could protect the escorted vessels,' recalled
Cadet Panayotis Analytis, who retained vivid memories of his days
in that torrid climate.

Life on board the *Averof* was anything but comfortable [he said
later]. My worst memories are of the unbearable heat which,
when combined with the high humidity, created an intolerable
situation. We cadets shared the midshipmen's quarters. But
because there were a lot of us, the most junior had to sleep on
hammocks in the corridor. The metal walls baked in the hot sun
and the air inside resembled a furnace.

The Greeks sweated so much that many developed ringworm
infections on the skin. Not surprisingly, they left most of the

hard coal stoking work to the Indians, though the cadets were also required to put in their hours of shovelling, which Analytis described as 'pure hell', from which they would emerge, their faces blackened with coal dust. Among the strangest sights Uncle George ever saw were Indian prayer mats on the decks with the stokers performing their religious duties in the shadow of the Christian guns. Haniotis remembered stoking duty as:

> ... long, backbreaking work that everyone had to do, regardless of rank. Even the second-in-command had to put on his overall. The only ones exempt were the ship's band members who played to keep up the spirits of those who toiled.

Others had kinder memories of life on board the *Averof* at Bombay. Leading Seaman Nikolaos Theologitis described the daily routine:

> What impressed me was the lax discipline. The food was good and the ingredients fresh. Our apparel was suited to the tropical climate. Our shore leave began right after the midday meal until 10 o'clock in the evening, with regular launch service. We were pretty much free to do what we wanted.

Captain Matesis (nicknamed Count Spyro for his genteel ways), influenced perhaps by his previous London posting as Greek naval attaché, would don his pressed whites every Saturday and go to the Bombay horseraces, taking groups of officers and petty officers with him. The British would hold a dance every Tuesday at the Taj Mahal hotel, and that, too, was a regular fixture for the *Averof*'s crew, as well as a weekly movie at the Radio City cinema, plus the posh Three Hundred Club in Calcutta where one could enter only in a dinner jacket. 'It was calm period,' recalled Chief Petty Officer (later Rear

Admiral) Alexander Ioannou, 'inside a colonial atmosphere which we tried to adjust to.' To Papasifakis, it was 'the British Empire in all its grandeur'.

Every Sunday the captain would have the crew on deck for inspection; the *Averof* by now was known for having discipline a degree stricter than on the RHN's smaller ships. It was, after all, the Greek flagship and the spit-and-polish element had to be rather more pronounced. The more junior cadets had to sleep in hammocks, leaving the cabins to the senior chief petty officers. When Papasifakis was finally able to get a cabin to himself, he found another occupant there – a mouse that would emerge from the air vent above his bunk every night and drop down on his prostrate form. He solved that problem by hanging a tin can lid from the vent; the lid rattled in the airflow and apparently scared the mouse away. 'Service on board a large ship,' wrote Papasifakis, 'is a great school for a young officer.'

One day Analytis, Alexandris and another cadet took advantage of some shore leave by engaging an old open-top cab driven by a white-turbaned Sikh. They wanted to go to see the hanging gardens of Cobala outside Bombay. On the way they passed a couple of fair-skinned and very attractive girls walking in the same direction, whom they took to be Europeans. They hadn't seen a woman in ages, so Analytis told the driver to stop and asked the girls in English if they cared to join the ride. By way of reply, as the other two were ogling the girls' bodies and muttering salaciously, one girl offered Analytis a carnation. Putting his nose to it, he said to the other two in Greek, 'It smells nice.'

'It certainly does,' the girl said – in perfect Greek. When Analytis got over the shock, the girls told him they were indeed Greek with British citizenship, the daughters of a family which had escaped the German invasion and had been shipped by the British to

India. What's more, the family had lived in the same Athens street as Analytis. Unfortunately, the source for this encounter tells us nothing of any result it might have had.

On another occasion a Dutch cruiser touched at Bombay, and when its officers saw the quaint shape of the *Averof* they clamoured to see 'the coal-burning ship from the past!' Wrote Papasifakis ruefully: 'It's a good thing they didn't ask us to do a stoking demonstration.' Another crowd of curiosity-seekers came in the form of Australian cadets on HMS *Exeter,* who were fascinated in their turn.[2]

In March 1942 Matesis was replaced. The new commander, Captain Nikolaos Petropoulos, could not have been a worse choice for the job. Petropoulos had the reputation of being a martinet and by all accounts was universally detested. One of the kinder comments made about him was that he was 'reclusive and eccentric'. Papasifakis portrayed him as 'tall, thin and dark, with a face lined with deep wrinkles (hence his nickname "Canyon-Face")'.

Petropoulos was actually a capable and clever man, but his unpleasant authoritarian streak tended to cancel out his better qualities. There were no doubts about his fighting spirit. He had messaged Sakellariou that his great ambition was 'to attack a Japanese cruiser and sink it'. That was admirable, but his single-minded Spartan-type insistence on grim duty and hardship grated seriously on everyone else. (Besides, old Uncle George would hardly have much chance against a new Japanese warship!) Petropoulos commanded the *Averof* for just three weeks, but no crewman had happy memories of that time. When taking command he stunned the assembled officer cadets by declaring that their main job was 'to clean the toilets'. In his eyes no-one could ever do anything right, and no rank was spared his insults. One day he issued an order for the arrest of an alleged deserter named Patronis who was believed to be at large in the steamy backstreets of Bombay. Leading Seaman

Gousis was part of a patrol sent out to find him. They discovered the deserter in a humble Indian dwelling, his face disfigured with signs of venereal disease. Back in chains on the *Averof*, Patronis was isolated in a tiny room without food and water. One evening Petropoulos ordered a sub lieutenant to beat the hapless seaman with a cudgel.

The officer, to his credit, refused. 'That, sir, runs counter to regulations,' he told the captain.

'Then come with me,' Petropoulos replied, 'and see how such people should be treated.' It was clear that he personally intended to administer the corporal punishment.

Standing by was Tsallis, an officer of the watch. 'What the hell,' he heard the sub lieutenant mutter as he reluctantly followed the captain. A short time later a posse of about three dozen seamen appeared on the foredeck carrying what looked like a heavy object. It was now dark and Tsallis, on watch, couldn't make out what it was. 'What's that you've got there?' he asked.

'It's Patronis, sir,' one of the seamen said. 'We think he's dead.'

'Get him to the sick bay at once!' Tsallis ordered. Some of the seamen, visibly enraged, made threatening moves on the officers' quarters, and Tsallis had some difficulty restraining them. 'If they had come on the captain at that moment,' Tsallis recalled, 'they'd have thrown him in the sea.' Some collapsed on the deck under the main gun turret and wept, while the chaplain and Tsallis tried to comfort them. 'When my brother was killed in Albania,' one seaman sobbed, 'I never cried as much as I've done with this f---ing commander.' Eventually Tsallis learned what had happened. Petropoulos had insisted on personally beating the already weakened and wretched Patronis while some of the bolder crewmembers pleaded with him not to do it. When the captain didn't listen, the pleas hardened into threats and insults. The torrent of abuse became so strong that Petropoulos, humiliated, gave up and fled to his quarters.

The following day, Petropoulos was nowhere to be seen. Patronis survived his ordeal, but that didn't make the crew's black mood any lighter. The senior officers didn't know what to do – keep the whole thing quiet and let it blow over or send a coded message to headquarters in Alexandria. They spent the day thinking it over, and in the morning of the next day Petropoulos appeared on deck as if nothing had happened. Tsallis overheard one seaman mutter to another: 'Look busy – the captain's here,' to which the reply came: 'Screw that piece of shit!' The officers waited all day for their commander to say something, but he went ashore for a couple of hours. When he came back he retreated to his cabin without a word. Tsallis and the others had decided to notify Alexandria when another officer suggested having it out personally with Petropoulos beforehand. Father Papanikolopoulos, the ship's chaplain, a figure of dignity in his black Orthodox robes and white beard, that evening gave vent to a quite unholy but understandable emotion:

> If that man [Petropoulos] had any ounce of self-respect he would jump into the sea and commit suicide. But not from this ship, for that way he would pollute the waters. He ought to get into an Indian dhow and go and drown himself farther out.

The meeting was set for 9.30 the following morning. Petropoulos insisted that each officer arrive singly to avoid attracting attention, and that there be no bugle call to signal the captain's conference. Petropoulos began by outlining the week's programme, as if nothing had happened. It was clear to Tsallis, for one, that 'Canyon Face' was evading the big issue. He rose and addressed the captain, excusing himself for speaking out of turn, and requested a transfer to another ship on the grounds that Petropoulos, despised by a large number of his crew, had forfeited his authority as commander of the *Averof*. The result, he said, was that discipline on board had broken down.

'Tsallis,' the captain replied evenly, 'it's nothing. Just give me 150 names of those who were on deck that night and I know what to do.'

'I am not the Gestapo to write down the names of 150 people unknown to me,' Tsallis shot back. 'There were no more than about fifty anyway. I cannot continue this conversation any more, sir.' Then he walked out. Shortly afterwards, Petropoulos went back ashore.

Later in the day Lieutenant Robert Swan, the Royal Navy liaison officer stationed on board, gave the crew more news. The Petropoulos incident had come to the attention of Rear Admiral Arthur Rattray, Flag Officer (Bombay) of the Royal Indian Navy and top naval commander in the area. An unrepentant Petropoulos had requested that the Royal Navy tow the *Averof* to a dockside so that all the 'mutineers' could be arrested, or failing that, sink the ship by shore fire – presumably with the crew still on board!

'Where do you sleep?' Rattray asked Petropoulos. 'On the ship or ashore?'

'Always on the ship, of course,' the Greek replied, a tad arrogantly.

'Well,' Rattray said, 'tonight you'll sleep in a hotel. Don't go back to collect your things, but send your batman.' Petropoulos had no choice but to obey.

Rattray ordered an unofficial enquiry by five Royal Navy ship commanders. Swan was present at the initial questioning, where Petropoulos exasperated the panel by evading every question and appearing not to realize his responsibilities. The unofficial enquiry ended by Rattray requesting the RHN headquarters in Alexandria to place Petropoulos in one month's pre-trial detention in Massawa jail.

Sakellariou in Alexandria acted fast, sending a captain named Perikles Antonopoulos to Bombay as commander of the RHN units in India and sword of justice. Tsallis was one of the first officers whom Antonopoulos interviewed, but at the end of the session the newly-arrived captain's face was sad. 'The trouble is,' he said, 'Sakellariou has ordered that all of you be punished.' That is, a good part of the *Averof*'s officer complement was going to share their skipper's blame. The next day a nasty Cypriot in a British army major's uniform began the interrogation. Legal snags soon arose. The Royal Navy pointed out that the Greeks had no authority to set up a naval court-martial in a foreign country; in India, only the Indian government could give permission for one, and that seemed unlikely. Meanwhile, the Indian press had got hold of the story and was plastering it over the front pages. More humiliation for the *Averof* and the RHN.

A Royal Navy officer flew to Alexandria to try and talk Sakellariou into softening his stand, but the Greek naval staff chief was adamant. In the end permission was given for the court-martial to be held at the British camp at Colaba, just south of Bombay. The Greek officers under indictment were not detained, but were confined to the *Averof*. The trial began on a sultry Monday morning towards the end of summer 1942 and lasted six days. Tsallis was one of twenty-eight officers accused of insubordination in the stormy meeting in the captain's quarters. They had no legal counsel; the single Greek lawyer to be found in Bombay had been engaged by Petropoulos. Tsallis had no doubts about the justice of his case. 'Our argument is that we acted in order to restore order to the ship and safeguard its prestige,' he told his twenty-seven fellow-accused. 'If you don't stick to that line you'll mess things up.' Swan said he was more than willing to testify on their behalf, if Rattray would let him.

Presiding over the court-martial was an RHAF group captain, Ioannis Kasimatis, flanked by an RHN commander and lieutenant commander. The obnoxious Cypriot major was the counsel for the prosecution, while defence counsel had been secured in the person of a lieutenant commander. Tsallis and the others were led in past a detachment of British sailors at parade rest, bayonets glinting on their rifles. Last of all, Petropoulos took his seat among the witnesses. Tsallis suspected that he sat near the accused in order to hear what they might say against him, or perhaps intimidate them by his proximity.

During the hearings Kasimatis, the airman, tried to be a fair and lenient judge. But the same cannot be said for the naval officers on the tribunal, who could not hide their detestation of the accused. Petropoulos often interrupted the proceedings to engage in flights of fancy, such as a bombastic assertion that the British hadn't built the defences of Bombay properly and hence he felt it his duty to 'defend the city with the *Averof*'. Not a few present thought the tropical heat had got to him. Tsallis was the last to testify. 'Tsallis, you're not afraid to tell the truth,' Group Captain Kasimatis said. 'Tell us exactly what happened.' When Tsallis finished his account, Swan rose.

'Sir,' he said, addressing the judge, 'I am here not just as a witness, but on the part of the admiral [Rattray], to say that the officers were not disloyal but did their duty.'

'What do you know about discipline?' one of the tribunal barked at him. Swan turned pale at the affront, about-faced and walked out of the room without another word. Kasimatis was visibly angry at the insult to Swan, but did nothing. 'We're not interested in what the British think,' the Cypriot prosecutor piped up. 'We are the ones judging.' No-one took the slightest notice of him. Tsallis could stand no more. Jumping from his seat, he addressed the tribunal president in a loud voice: 'Permission to speak, sir!' Kasimatis gave it. The Cypriot repeated his dismissive remark about the opinion of the British.

> But we officers who every day enter Colaba [Tsallis said], would very much like to know what the British think. Because if we are convicted in the knowledge that the British opposed the decision of the court-martial, when we're in jail we'll at least have the satisfaction of knowing it.

That was the trigger for the Cypriot prosecutor to spew out a torrent of invective against Tsallis personally, ending with a demand for the death penalty for him. Tsallis was quite expecting it, but had faith in Kasimatis as a reasonable man. The verdicts were announced in the afternoon of the trial's final day. Tsallis was the first to be sentenced, to six months in jail. He later wrote that the time lapse between the words 'six' and 'months' issuing from the judge's lips seemed like a century.

He was one of the luckier ones. Six of the accused were given life sentences, and nineteen others twenty years. The convicted men were sent to a jail at Nazik, 120 miles north of Bombay. The Greeks were given the best cells, each man to a cell. Second class was reserved for jailed members of Mahatma Gandhi's banned Congress Party, while Indian common criminals were crammed into third class. Tsallis did not find it terribly unpleasant. He and the others appreciated the exercise periods, when they were allowed to stroll beneath the shade of the trees and watch squirrels scurrying up and down them. Two lower-ranking Greek inmates were on hand to serve as batmen. One of the *Averof*'s cooks was sent to rustle up daily European meals, as few could stomach the jail's Indian fare. Tsallis mused that he and his friends were perhaps 'the first white men to snap the chains of colonialism and enter an Indian jail'.

Kasimatis and Swan made a point of visiting them and keeping their spirits up. The group captain wryly noted a parallel with Socrates, jailed and put to death undeservedly in ancient Athens for a noble cause. Kasimatis wondered what Sakellariou's reaction would be when he returned to Alexandria to give a full report of the trial and verdict. As for Swan, horrified at the predicament of his Greek comrades, he was continually in tears and could not speak. The inmates received letters of encouragement from the midshipmen of the *Averof*, all of whom had been confined below decks for four months in the torrid heat, locked in their darkened cabins. The perpetrator of this atrocity was Commander George Zeppos, a former submarine commander with a good war record, but hardly a humanitarian, in temporary command of the *Averof* after Petropoulos' removal (and subsequent trial and conviction for cruelty).

A month into their sentence, the inmates had a visit from the Greek consul in Bombay who brandished a sheet of paper. 'Sign this,' he told the officers, 'and you'll go free.' The paper was a formal statement of repentance, with places for thirty signatures. Tsallis refused to sign and treated the consul to a stern lecture on how his own actions had accorded with the highest moral and patriotic motives. Despite the fact that he, Tsallis, had left aged relations and dependants in Athens, he had nonetheless come away with the *Averof* to fight. 'Does this not prove, Mr Consul, that I have always been willing to serve my country?' Hearing Tsallis' speech, the others refused to sign as well. The consul departed expressionless, though Tsallis later learned that he admired such an indomitable spirit. When their prison terms were completed, the officers walked out of the Nazik jail, their 'heads high'.

Zeppos' reign, too, was brief. Sakellariou had the good sense to send out the gentlemanly Captain Matesis, Petropoulos' immediate predecessor, to regain command of the *Averof*. From that moment, normal life returned to the ship. As for Tsallis, he realized his career in the Greek navy was over, and so Rattray gave him a choice between the Royal Navy and the Royal Indian Navy. The latter had a greater need of officers, and so in a matter of days Tsallis found himself in a classroom familiarizing himself with newfangled devices such as Asdic (anti-submarine detection) and the nuances of the English language. He was appointed a lieutenant on board the 2,800-ton HMIS *Sonavati*, serving with the RIN for the rest of the war.[3]

As life on the *Averof* settled back to normal, Lieutenant Swan, having recovered from his emotional shock after the trial, set time aside for the swimming pools and tennis courts, impressing the excitable Greeks and bringing some equilibrium back into their spirits – which may well have been reservist Swan's biggest contribution to the war effort in the Far East.

But one thing could not be reversed, and that was Uncle George's age. When the ship moved out into the bay for gunnery trials, the blasts dislodged two of the 17-year-old Belleville boilers and sent them crashing to the floor. Several other boilers had been worn out and deactivated for years. In the eyes of the Royal Navy, Uncle George was spending so much time under repair at Bombay that British wags took to dubbing it the *Never-off*. That sarcasm rankled. 'Our smart and beloved cruiser was humbled through no fault of its own,' wrote Tsallis. 'Its heart was certainly hurt.' For those who believe that ships have souls, it was a telling comment.

Some thought was naturally given to how to increase Uncle George's speed. Tsallis served as the captain's interpreter in a meeting with John Illingworth, an engineer officer on HMS *Glasgow*, and five other British officers. Since its refit in France in the 1920s, the *Averof* had used an oil-fired system to ignite the coal more quickly. The system had been somewhat improved at Port

Sudan. Illingworth suggested a refinement, but in the end nothing happened, as the projected speed benefits were judged to be not worth the effort and expense.

After three convoy escorts, the *Averof*'s usefulness to the Allied war effort was judged to be over. It sailed back to Port Said, where it arrived in mid-November 1942. By now the British Eighth Army had halted General Erwin Rommel's Afrika Korps in its tracks at El Alamein and Egypt was secure. The *Averof* remained at Port Said as the Greek flagship. Stopping at Port Tewfiq, the ship had received word that Crown Prince Paul and his wife Frederica were planning to visit. The layers of coal dust clinging to the superstructure were frantically scrubbed away, but couldn't be cleaned from the crew's faces in time, with the result that the royal visitors were surprised by the unnaturally dark skins on parade. It wasn't just sunburn.

Meanwhile Sakellariou had been bombarding his prime minister with incessant pessimistic memos about the state of the navy. The memos had had their result, but not the one he expected. The fleet commander, Rear Admiral Kavvadias, was named undersecretary for the navy and Sakellariou appointed fleet commander in addition to his job as navy minister, a curious juxtaposition of ranking that only served to confuse policymaking. He was convinced that he was being made a scapegoat for incompetence and corruption at the top, but nonetheless felt that he had to continue serving his country, whatever the obstacles. This was before Rommel had been stopped at El Alamein and at the end of June 1942 the RHN had quit Alexandria for Port Said. Sakellariou, ill in hospital at the time, had to be moved on a stretcher.

When the *Averof* returned from India in November, Sakellariou moved his headquarters back on board, while ensuring that training continued to turn out an appreciable number of officers and petty officers. He received a boost from Vice Admiral Henry Harwood, Admiral Sir Andrew Cunningham's successor as the Royal Navy commander in the Mediterranean, who thanked the Greek admiral for keeping his crews under control and away from subversion. That happy situation, however, was not to last, as Tsouderos and the king continued to intrigue against Sakellariou. He was listening to the BBC on the evening of 24 March 1943 when the news reader intoned that his 'resignation' from the post of RHN fleet commander had been 'accepted'! That *fait accompli* came as a total shock, quite out of the blue, and there was absolutely nothing he could do about it. Three days later he boarded an American military aircraft in Cairo to fly to America on a diplomatic mission, effectively putting him out of the way. His career with the navy, which fittingly had begun and ended on the *Averof*, was essentially over.

There were a few inspiring moments to break the general gloom. On 22 October 1943 the RHN destroyer *Adrias* hit a mine off Kalymnos. The blast tore off the ship's entire bow section, but its skipper, Commander Ioannis Toumbas, ignored British orders to abandon the badly crippled ship and after emergency repairs in a Turkish port, sailed it to Alexandria in early December. Cadet Alexandris was there to see the triumphant entry of the bow-less *Adrias*, its wound gaping horribly, already dubbed by the press 'the ship that wouldn't die'.

> The port was crowded with people [Alexandris recalled]. All the ships there, warships and merchantmen of every nationality, were bedecked with flags and hooting, their crews paraded on the deck. There are no words to describe it. The salvage tugs threw up fountains of water while the crews cheered. It was a glorious day for our Navy.

'What a reception!' wrote Doxiadis, now an acting midshipman, who was also on hand to view the spectacle. 'The place went crazy ... There were tears in my eyes and my hair stood on end from emotion.' Toumbas was decorated with the Greek Gold Medal for Valour and Military Cross Third Class, while the Royal Navy overlooked his refusal to obey an order and got him awarded the Distinguished Service Order.

With the strong hand of Sakellariou out of the way, the stage was set for some of the darkest days the Royal Hellenic Navy had to face – not from the guns and planes of the enemy but from some of its own people, twisted into instruments of hate by the burgeoning communist movement. The year 1942 had seen the emergence in Greece of resistance guerrilla movements which were soon brought under the ruthless control of the Greek Communist Party (KKE), which itself was an instrument of Soviet leader Josef Stalin. The glamour of resistance fighting had burnished the KKE's image, and thus it was inevitable that bolshevik sentiment should spread to the Greek servicemen in Egypt. Many had been inactive for months while the British did the bulk of the fighting. The Greek government-in-exile in London had become notorious for its cronyism and corruption; the comfortable life of senior Greek officers in Alexandria and Cairo was an insult to those less well-connected. In the RHN, the result exploded on 2 April 1944 when the crews of several Greek ships formed 'soviets' on the bolshevik model and proceeded to mutiny along lines prepared well in advance by the KKE and Moscow.

The revolt took Rear Admiral Kavvadias, the navy undersecretary and head of the RHN, by surprise, but so far advanced was the unrest that he could at first do little about it. The KKE had managed to infiltrate a chief agitator into the *Averof*'s crew in the form of a petty officer responsible for the magazine. This man had the keys to the magazine and therefore could control the ship's firepower. The officers initially had orders to be lenient on offenders; but in the view of some, this only encouraged the dissident elements in their disobedience. A month previously, three Greek-speaking British officers, trained in intelligence work, had been appointed to the *Averof* ostensibly as interpreters but in reality to assess the growing security risk.

The mutiny on the *Averof* broke out on 4 April, when a communist action committee – all armed with pistols and hand grenades – distributed a document calling on all the crew to sign a proclamation that the ship, once it returned to Greek waters, would place itself under the command of the communist resistance army. Many were intimidated into signing. When the document reached Captain Andreas Golemis, who had replaced Matesis, he angrily threw the bearers out of his quarters. In reprisal, the rebels sent two armed seamen to keep him a prisoner in his own cabin before banishing him ashore. The committee leaders took over the well-appointed stern cabin which had been the quarters of Admiral Koundouriotis in the Balkan Wars. A loyal petty officer named George Imellos had been allowed to enter the captain's quarters on some errand, when he saw Golemis gesturing to him surreptitiously and putting a finger to his lips.

'I don't need you for anything, Imellos,' the captain whispered, visibly emotional. 'Before I go I just want to shake your hand because you're a true Greek.'

'You may be going, sir,' Imellos replied, 'but here they're pressuring me to sign that document. If they threaten to shoot me and I'm forced to sign, will I have your support?'

'You shouldn't be asking that question,' Golemis said. 'I'm not signing, but then I'm not you. I'm the commander.' The captain's eyes filled with tears as he squeezed Imellos' hand again. A few hours later Golemis and his number two were seen off the ship, accompanied by a parody of a guard of honour. Imellos 'felt like an orphan'. The standard of the rebel resistance army was hoisted on the mainmast. A certain Commander George Stamatopoulos was believed to be the chief mutineer, but real power lay in the hands of the communist ideologues who served as sub lieutenants and petty officers. The crew were talked – or intimidated – into giving up their weapons, which were placed under lock and key.

Another loyal crewmember, Ordinary Seaman George Antippas, found himself hustled into a dark cell in the bowels of the ship. Alone in the dark, he spent a day there, listening to the rats 'as big as cats' scuttling around him. Towards evening he heard a man calling for someone who could speak English. 'I can,' Antippas shouted, and soon he found himself back in daylight, receiving orders from the mutineers' committee to be the *Averof*'s point man at the Royal Navy headquarters at Port Said, which was coordinating the night's anti-aircraft barrage plans.

There was no raid that night, and by dawn the next morning Antippas was one of the few crewmembers not asleep. This was a chance for him to escape the communist-controlled ship and get ashore, if he could elude the guards who patrolled the main decks with machine guns, ready to shoot any 'rightwing reactionary monarchist' trying to escape. Going down rather than up, Antippas squeezed through a porthole of the crews' latrines just above the waterline, slipped into the water and swam the 100 metres to shore without being detected. Almost naked – he'd had to doff most of his clothes to get through the porthole – he got to the Greek Yacht Club in Port Said where he telephoned for rescue. Soon, wrapped in a blanket helpfully provided by a club porter named Gamal, Antippas was safe in Alexandria.

About ten days later Imellos secured permission to go ashore at Port Said, where he bought and donned a civilian suit, carried his uniform in a bag and went to the home of a Greek doctor where he found the chaplain, Father Papanikolopoulos, and another *Averof* officer deep in conversation. The Greek government-in-exile had just issued a stern order to the rebels to cease their subversion. The rebels had jeered, forcing the resignation of prime minister Tsouderos. He was replaced by Sophokles Venizelos, a son of the statesman Eleftherios Venizelos who had played a large part in acquiring the *Averof* in 1911.

The RHN command now decided to deal firmly with the nastiness. Imellos and others who had escaped the *Averof*'s 'people's republic' had gathered at Port Said to form an operations office under the command at Alexandria. One day Golemis called the office and ordered its personnel to prepare for transfer to Alexandria. What Golemis did not add, doubtless for reasons of security, was that the RHN was planning to take back control of its ships by force. On 14 April a captain named Constantine Skoufopoulos was appointed to command the *Averof*. As soon as he set foot on board, the rebels arrested him. The Royal Navy, which had been supplying the Greek ships throughout, cut off the provisioning. The rebels ordered the crews of the smaller communist-controlled ships to assemble on the *Averof*, where the rebel committee used megaphones to appeal to the Red Cross to supply food and water – otherwise, the ship would be sunk right in the entrance to the Suez Canal, blocking it. The British dealt with that threat by sending the RAF to buzz the cruiser and wreath it in smoke screens. Two RN torpedo boats would play mind games by speeding directly at the ship, as if to launch torpedoes, and then veer off at the last minute. Two British cruisers took up positions on either side of the *Averof*, swivelling their guns in gunnery practice, sometimes aiming them right at the cruiser.

The rebels' resolve soon crumbled. About ten days into the crisis Antippas found himself part of an assault team on board the Royal

Navy cruiser HMS *Ajax*, charged with reclaiming the *Averof* for its rightful command. Also on board was Captain Golemis. When the team arrived at Port Said Imellos wanted to join, but Golemis kept him on the administration side out of harm's direct way. 'You'll fight with your pen,' the captain said, and Imellos was set to registering everyone who was given a weapon from the British armoury. (Once he finished that, he grabbed a weapon like everyone else.) Officers and men in no particular order piled into the landing craft that would take them to the *Averof*, moored about a mile offshore. 'Rank didn't count,' Imellos recalled. 'We were all soldiers.'

The British gave the rebels an hour in which to give themselves up. The committee asked for six hours to consider the ultimatum after which, if the rebels were to capitulate, they were to do so to the British and not to the Greeks; moreover, they ought to be allowed to parade with red banners flying, singing their communist resistance songs. The British rejected the request out of hand. Nevertheless the rebels insisted – knowing with what tender mercies the Greek government forces would handle them – on being taken off the ship by British launches. Meanwhile, the rebel committee had ordered that any loyalist seamen found hiding on the *Averof* should be shot on the spot. RN launches duly removed the rebels. That left the task of determining which of the detained seamen were actually communists or sympathizers. Most, in fact, had been compelled at gunpoint to adhere to the cause. After careful questioning, it turned out that at least 80 per cent of the 'rebels' were unwilling accomplices and given pardons. The hardline minority were trucked to desert detention camps.

The first loyal officer to board the *Averof* was Commander Ilias Veriopoulos, whose first order to a seaman was, 'Get that rag off and throw it away.' That 'rag' was the emblem of the communist-controlled ELAN organization, known to its adherents as the

'People's Navy,' which had been hoisted in place of the national flag. As the seaman complied he heard muttered threats from the last of the rebels being led away.

Golemis, though, had seen the last of his ship. Though he had acted impeccably throughout the crisis, displaying commendable courage under duress, the naval staff felt that a change of command would help clear the political air. Kavvadias' choice to head the *Averof* was Captain Panayotis Konstas, a battle-hardened officer who, as commander of the destroyer *Psara* early in the war, had shelled Italian positions on the Albanian coast.

The communist-led mutiny had been especially severe in Alexandria. After mobs of mutineers besieged the Cadets' College in Alexandria on 4 April, the Royal Navy had to step in, banning all Greek military personnel from the streets without special permission and clearing out the mutineers from occupied buildings at gunpoint. The following day, the commander and officers of the destroyer *Pindos* were thrown overboard. A communist seaman sneaked up behind Moschos, sitting at his desk on board the destroyer *Kriti*, and shot him in the back. Sub Lieutenant Nikolaos Roussen, a classmate and ex-*Averof* crewmember, held Moschos' head as he was rushed to hospital; Roussen himself was later killed by a burst of machine gun fire from one of his own men. Moschos survived, his left upper arm shattered, but he never found out who shot him.

The prevailing curious stance of the mutineers has been described as 'stylized disobedience' by Moschos. It became the practice for every order from an officer to an enlisted man to be directly challenged and, after this ritual defiance was uttered, the subordinate would mutter sullenly, 'whatever you order, sir,' and the order would be carried out. Naturally, this theatrical and infantile bolshevism got seriously on the nerves of the senior officers and baffled and alarmed the British. On some ships, officers' side-arms were confiscated. Cadet Alexandris was in his final year at Alexandria when the insurrectionists tried to take over the college premises. The cadets themselves rallied and, with just a few exceptions, helped the navy leadership regain control of the college and ships in a counterattack in the early hours of 23 April. This was the operation in which Roussen died, as well as Sub Lieutenant Dimitrios Reppas, who happened to be the son of Air Vice Marshal George Reppas, a former commander of the Royal Hellenic Air Force.

Admiral Cunningham, now the Allied commander in the Mediterranean, warned Kavvadias that the Greek navy was disintegrating. He was furious that a lack of Greek escort ships, immobilized by the mutiny, had resulted in the torpedoing of an American troopship with large loss of life. President Roosevelt himself was livid. If the Greek navy leadership allowed the subversion to continue, Cunningham warned, then the RHN would no longer be considered a reliable fighting force. Yet Cunningham hesitated to use the force of British arms to quell the Greek mutiny. First, it would hand a huge propaganda coup to the Germans, and second, it would create an anti-British undercurrent of feeling in Greece that would only benefit the communist cause and Stalin's schemes. In the end, diplomatic handling by the fleet commander, Rear Admiral Constantine Alexandris, defused the worst tensions. But the bad feeling and militant bolshevism were by no means extinguished.

By now the *Averof* was down to barely a couple of hundred effectives, from a pre-mutiny complement of some 1,100 men. But it was the end of summer 1944, the Axis was losing on all fronts, and it was becoming clear that the liberation of Greece from the Germans could not long be delayed. The *Averof,* with order restored among its crew, sailed from Port Said to Alexandria together with the destroyers *Aetos, Ierax* and *Panthir* to load supplies and equipment for the expected return to Greece. There was also the delicate issue of replacing the Indian stokers, as in the mood of the time, some high-ranking chaps didn't want Uncle George to return to Greece with 120 foreign-looking coloured crewmen on board. Even those Greeks whose faces were chronically blackened with coal dust were actually told to lie low until they could lighten up! A happy omen was the appointment of Captain Theodore Koundouriotis, the son of the renowned admiral, as commander of the ship.

On 13 October, the day after the last German troops rode out of Athens, Uncle George set out on his triumphant voyage back home, appropriately dubbed 'Operation Manna'. The crew was suffused with expectant joy. Sailing alongside was the heroic *Adrias*, still with its bow missing. But there were many square miles of German mines yet to be cleared, and two RHN minesweepers, the *Kos* and the *Kasos*, hit mines and sank, along with two British vessels. Koundouriotis judged it prudent to stop at the island of Poros to allow the approaches to Piraeus to be completely cleared. At Poros the ship received a visit from the new Greek prime minister, George Papandreou. Midshipman Nikolaos Syxeris was deputed to meet Papandreou and escort him on board. When the two met, the prime minister kissed the officer three times on both cheeks, saying 'Our country,' each time.

That same afternoon the grand old cruiser, with Papandreou and several dignitaries on board and a Koundouriotis again in command, sailed for Piraeus. Syxeris was put in charge of the launch that took the prime minister ashore. Papandreou seems to have felt that to associate himself with Greece's prime symbol of naval prestige would boost his authority in Athens. For that authority was coming under serious threat.

As many homecoming crewmembers discovered, after more than three years of Axis occupation and resistance fighting Greece had become a very different place from what it was in spring 1941.

Syxeris recoiled in horror at the central Piraeus commuter train station where he came on the mangled remains of some 300 Italian soldiers. The retreating Germans had tied explosives to them and blown them up. Grimness and violence were in the air.

Midshipman Apostolos Evangelopoulos went ashore to see if his home and family were still where he had left them. In the streets he found universal relief that the Germans had left, but a relief tinged with fear of what had replaced them – militant groups of communist-led 'people's police' who seemed to be everywhere. These were the outgrowth of the Greek resistance movement, which had grown under communist control to become a real threat to the leadership of the war-shattered country. The port of Piraeus, for example, was completely under the control of ELAN. While the RHN had been helping the British as best it could in the Middle East and in India, the ELAN had been busy through the German occupation in preparing the ground for a seizure of power, along with its more powerful land-based equivalent, the ELAS. Their aim: to abolish the monarchy and western-style parliamentary democracy and drag Greece into the communist orbit of the then Soviet Union.

'Watch yourselves when you go ashore,' Koundouriotis had warned his crewmembers. 'Keep your lips tight and don't be conspicuous.' Evangelopoulos couldn't help thinking back to the delirious national joy when Greece had entered the war in October 1940, and contrasting it with the desolate and fearful atmosphere prevailing now. Red flags flew from balconies everywhere and the streets were eerily silent. Imellos, after literally stooping to kiss his native soil at Piraeus, made his way to the Athens suburb where he had lived before the war. His girlfriend, whom he hadn't seen for four years, was sitting waiting for him on the front step of his house. Her family had become so poor during the German occupation that she had cut up a handbag to make into a pair of shoes.[4]

Chapter 10

Retirement and Rats

The *Averof* spent the year of grace 1945 settling down at its old mooring at the Salamis naval station, as its veterans swapped yarns of the Middle East and India, much as Alexander the Great's salty seamen must have done in the fourth century BC. In that year it paid prestige visits to Thessaloniki and Rhodes to mark the accession of the Dodecanese islands to Greece. Back at Salamis Uncle George was given the honour of serving as RHN fleet headquarters, a job which kept him more or less out of danger as the pessimists' fears came true and Greece underwent four more years of conflict in the form of a devastating civil war.

Less than two months after the *Averof* returned home, the communists attempted to seize power. Through December 1944 they were beaten back in vicious street fighting in Athens, with British army and RAF help. Though the shaky national government under Papandreou just held on, and George II was back in his palace with British and American support, the communists formed a large rebel army and continued the fight in the mountains of central and northern Greece, causing untold misery and death until they were stamped out in September 1949 and Greece finally had a chance to stagger back on its feet.

In 1951 the Greek state was judged stable enough to become a member of Nato. That was also the year that the *Averof* completed forty years of active service – a good opportunity to finally decommission the heroic old armoured cruiser, at last thoroughly deserving of an honoured retirement. But what was that retirement actually to be? The ship's fighting value was, of course, zero. Money for upkeep was not plentiful, while the RHN was acquiring newer vessels from the Americans. There were, of course, calls for Uncle George to finally submit to the scrap yard, but here again Saint Nicholas seemed to stretch forth his protective hand. In the post-war years many countries were scrapping excess warship tonnage, and the resulting glut in the scrap market had seriously depressed prices. There were, of course, those who argued to preserve the ship at any cost, and for several years the defence ministry could come to no decision. A way of evading the issue was found in 1957 by towing the *Averof* to the offshore island of Poros and mooring it in front of the island's petty officers' school as a floating gate guard.

In those years the Greek islands were taking their first steps towards becoming popular holiday destinations. Poros, just a few hours' leisurely cruise from Piraeus, was particularly easy to reach. Through the 1950s and 1960s island-hopping boats would round the northern headland of Poros, coming in from Aigina or Methana, and there the *Averof* would greet them, its pale grey hull contrasting oddly with the hosts of small white yachts and fishing boats puttering around it. But old warships were not considered tourist attractions in those days, especially in the 'make love not war' era, and generations of holidaymakers would spare no more than a passing glance at the hulk as they strolled to the beaches and seaside tavernas. Even the locals didn't appear to be much interested in it.

The petty officers in training might regard the *Averof* as a static museum piece, but security was pretty much nonexistent. As tourists arrived in ever greater numbers each summer, Uncle George became, in the words of one authority, 'the victim of souvenir-hunters who removed anything that was not firmly screwed down.' The interior 'gradually [decayed] into a succession of damp, rusty caverns infested by gigantic rats'.[1] Almost everything that could be vandalized was, from the small chapel to Koundouriotis' opulent wood-panelled quarters. The only visible sign that some rudimentary care was being taken was a new coat of grey paint now and then. And so the *Averof* remained for twenty-seven years, awaiting the day when it would rust to bits.

During that time, politics in Greece had been as turbulent as ever. In April 1967 a trio of Greek army colonels staged a highly efficient and almost bloodless coup d'etat, ending a period in which vengeful partisan politics had come close to paralysing the country. The coup ringleader was Colonel George Papadopoulos, who for the next six years would administer a military-backed dictatorial regime as Greece's strongman. Papadopoulos had the blessings of the Americans and NATO, who had never ceased worrying that Greece might fall into the Soviet bloc. The Papadopoulos regime sanctified all things military and tried to raise public consciousness of the Greek glories of the past, of which the *Averof* was an integral part. In early 1973 the naval staff allocated the equivalent of £30,000 to spruce up the armoured cruiser. It was sixty years after the Battle of Limnos, and to mark the anniversary Papadopoulos sent more than a hundred technicians to repair the results of sixteen years of neglect. The objective was to move the *Averof* from Poros to Piraeus and turn it into a floating museum.

But political events in that year thwarted the move, as the military-backed dictatorship was showing signs of strain. As had happened so often in Greece's recent history, coups and dictatorships had been almost exclusively army affairs, with the navy and air force relegated to the sidelines. Though the RHN was kept under tight control, many senior, middle and lower-ranking officers cultivated a secret democratic tradition seen as going right back to Themistokles and the ancient Athenian democrats who manned the triremes in the Persian and Peloponnesian Wars. In fact, almost from day one of the coup, RHN officers had begun plotting against Papadopoulos. The unofficial ringleader was Commander Nikolaos Pappas, a thick-set, intense officer, whose varied schemes included a plot to kidnap Papadopoulos as he was at sea observing naval wargames and seize Crete as a rebel base. The regime's efficient military police scotched both plots.

Public opposition to Papadopoulos and his government, at home and abroad, got bolder. In March 1973 students at the Athens University law school began demonstrating. This was the signal for Pappas, who had been honing an ambitious plan to use a NATO exercise, during which many ships would be at sea and hence hard to control, to topple Papadopoulos. The plan harked back to the feverish days of 1935; the first move would be to seize the island of Syros as a base from which two squadrons would sail, one to Piraeus and the other to Thessaloniki to isolate the main cities and force the junta to step down – with gunfire if necessary. The operation was scheduled to begin at 2.00 am on 23 May 1973.

But the junta's security services were too quick for Pappas. Conspirator security had been spotty at best. Two days before the scheduled start, Pappas received a call from his friends in navy headquarters that the plot had been busted and several conspirators arrested. This left Pappas little choice but to make a getaway in the ship he commanded, the destroyer *Velos*, on the pretence of taking part in a NATO naval exercise west of Italy. The *Velos*, in fact, was the only RHN vessel to escape, while the Papadopoulos regime took to the airwaves to deride the naval conspiracy as 'a piece of comic opera', which admittedly was not far off the mark.

The *Velos* arrived off Fiumicino, south of Rome, on 25 May. Pappas at once sought to make international media capital out of his exploit, claiming that most of his crew was on his side. At the same time he signalled NATO headquarters that he was defecting out of respect for the provisions of the North Atlantic Treaty which is designed to 'safeguard the freedom of [the members'] peoples ... on the principles of democracy, individual liberty and the rule of law'. In Pappas' view, as the Papadopoulos regime had been flouting those principles for six years, the RHN's participation in the exercises ran counter to the treaty. That, however, was mere cover for the plain fact that his conspiracy was an utter failure. He knew he would be seized if he returned to Greece; defection was his only way out. Before the assembled press and newsreel cameras at Fiumicino, Pappas, six officers and twenty-five petty officers asked for political asylum in Italy. According to later accounts, the rest of the crew were deterred from doing likewise for fear of reprisals against their families back home; but equally likely, they simply didn't care to oppose the regime. These latter returned with the ship to Salamis a month later.

The immediate effect of Pappas' failed navy plot was to strengthen Papadopoulos' position at home. The strongman suspected that King Constantine II – in exile in Rome since an abortive counter-coup in December 1967 – had secretly backed the plot, and so in June 1973 he abolished the Greek monarchy and proclaimed a republic. The Royal Hellenic Navy, now the plain Hellenic Navy, resumed its position as a faithful pillar of the military-backed government. Yet within months, Pappas's gesture had unexpectedly dramatic consequences. Student unrest exploded anew in November 1973, forcing the regime to crack down with tanks. Papadopoulos found himself toppled from power by an even harsher military dictator who in turn fell after an ill-advised military adventure in Cyprus in July 1974. The upshot was that on 23 July the regime cashed in its chips and agreed to the restoration of parliamentary democracy. The colonels' seven-year rule was over, and bloodlessly, too.

In October 1981 Greece's first-ever socialist government was elected. One of its first acts was promote Pappas to vice admiral and appoint him chief of staff of the HN. Though the appointment was made for obvious political reasons, as a reward of sorts for his action with the *Velos* nearly twenty years before, Pappas did have several original ideas. One of them, ironically, was to revive the junta's plan of 1973 and rescue the *Averof* from slow oblivion at Poros, to restore it as a historic ship worthy of preservation. One bright day in 1984 the old ship was tugged loose from its mooring at Poros (some of the locals, admittedly, did feel a sense of loss at its going) and towed stern-first to its old home at Salamis where it was dry-docked to see if its hull was still intact. It was found to be quite sound – the 70-year-old 200mm Krupp steel plating had withstood the years magnificently. All the ship needed was a fresh coat of paint, and thus dolled up, the *Averof* was put on display at Zea, a popular yacht marina at the Piraeus waterfront, for Navy Week 1984. It was an instant hit, with 60,000 people going on board in a single week. Pappas' hunch – that the disco-dancing and unmilitary younger generation would take to the *Averof* as eagerly as older generations – proved correct. The government's three decades of indecision were over: the *Averof* was going to be restored, and properly.

Chapter 11

Comeback

The years passed and Uncle George was painstakingly spruced up while he took up a new mooring at Flisvos yacht marina, less than half a mile from the posh apartment buildings, offices and cafés lining the Phaleron coast road and in the company of the latest floating acquisitions of the wealthy. Admiral Koundouriotis' sumptuous quarters were restored to their previous wood-panelled and crystalline splendour, while exhibits were transferred on board from the Hellenic Maritime Museum. The decks also began to re-live something of the glitter of the days in Constantinople; ship-owners would host summer cocktail parties on board, with a wink (possibly oiled with bribes) from the naval authorities. From war-winner to workhorse to museum, the *Averof* was about to complete its century as an occasional stamping ground for tuxedos, cigars, short skirts and high heels. In June 2010, however, the phenomenon got out of hand.

It all seemed respectable enough when it was reported that the organizers of an international shipping exhibition intended to hold an exhibitors' reception on board. That report, however, appears to have been intended to mislead the public about the real purpose of the event which was to celebrate the wedding of a wealthy Greek shipowner to a top-market fashion model and television personality. The *Averof*'s decks had already been the stage for media events such as a breakfast television programme with aerobics in 1996 and another party organized by the same shipowning family in June 2008. But when pictures of this latest gala appeared in the press, featuring scantily-clad girls sitting atop the Vickers guns, the storm broke.

The first protest came from Emmanuel Kefaloyannis, a Cretan conservative member of parliament who saw a chance to score a point against Greece's socialist government of the time. According to Kefaloyannis, 'converting a living memorial of modern Greek history into a nightclub' was a stain on the defence ministry's reputation. 'It is shameful,' the deputy said, 'that we should be prisoners of the power and frivolousness of rich people.' The defence minister, Evangelos Venizelos (no relation to the prime minister of a hundred years before), fielded the ball the only way a politician could in the circumstances, by beating his breast more loudly than anyone. Terming the party 'a deep affront to the honour of the navy and our patriotic sensibility,' Venizelos sacked the *Averof*'s commander-cum museum curator, Commodore Eleftherios Gavalas, and Greece's tycoons, it was felt, were duly put in their place. The shipowning family itself professed astonishment at the reaction, especially as it claimed it had contributed funds for the armoured cruiser's restoration. Moreover, the family added, no-one had protested at the identical 2008 shipboard dance, so what was all the fuss about?

The fuss was essentially about the crunching Greek economic crisis, then in its second year. Greek shipowners, as epitomizing the global rich, were not exactly the media's favourite people, and the politicians capitalized on that feeling. Among the bulk of the Greek public a pre-World War Two atmosphere was simmering, with Germany again the villain – this time imposing a harsh economic rule on Greece on the pretext of saving the euro in cahoots with other global powers such as the International Monetary Fund. Moreover, the country's armed forces were suffering a series of cuts. Public opinion felt subliminally that something of Greece's glory – besides the Parthenon and ancient monuments – ought to be preserved as a reminder that Greece once made her foes tremble, that a century ago the *Averof*'s black smoke and belching guns commanded respect in the Aegean Sea. One journalist, answering those who judged Venizelos' reaction excessive, wrote in his blog:

> How many of us, and of those who partied on its decks … remember the events that proved this ship to be the ark of national struggles, so that we can treat it with the respect it deserves? The laid-up *Averof* is a symbol that was born in a Livorno shipyard … and since 11 September 1911 when it sailed into Phaleron (to an enthusiastic welcome), to begin its voyage through all the wars of our stormy modern history, it has ended up today, moored at a jetty in Phaleron, officially a museum but unofficially a dance floor.[1]

When the sun shines on the yacht-studded blue expanse of Phaleron Bay, Uncle George receives his daily stream of visitors. Legions of schoolchildren gaze in awe at the great guns pointing at the horizon, the preserved hammocks of the crew and the ornate decor of the wardroom. Digital cameras and smartphones click away in the quiet compartments where once officers' commands echoed and the steel walls vibrated with the surge of the great Ansaldo engines – still in working order. Shovel enough coal down the chutes and the *Averof* can sail again. It probably won't, though, because the belching black smoke would inevitably give rise to protests from those who would fail to see the 'significance' of the event. And the carbon footprint – something unknown in simpler and more heroic times – would be an issue of some concern.

Whenever a warship enters Phaleron Bay and is about to pass in front of the *Averof,* the warship commander gives the order: 'Face armoured cruiser *Averof,* attention port [or starboard]!' That's the signal for the officer complement to assemble on deck and stand to attention, saluting Uncle George. The ritual is more than just paying homage to a great ship; like the stained powder bucket inside, it's a recognition that probably something higher than human agency has enabled RHNS *Averof* to be still with us.

Notes and References

Prologue
1. Jonathan Swift, *Gulliver's Travels* (Boston; Houghton Mifflin Riverside Editions 1960) p. 7.

Chapter 1
1. 'The Mysterious Mr Zedzed: The Wickedest Man in the World', *Past Imperfect, Smithsonian Magazine* (16 Feb 2012).
2. Recent research indicates that it may have been considerably less, given Zaharoff's lavish endowments and donations, plus losses from his almost certain financial backing of the abortive Greek drive to eject the Turks from Asia Minor in 1920–22.
3. Katsouros' diary gives no indication of his actual rank. A photograph of him taken at some distance, on the deck of the *Averof,* shows a single band of gold braid around his sleeve; therefore I feel justified in assigning him the rank of sub lieutenant. The elegant style of his handwriting would also argue for officer status at that time.

Chapter 2
1. *Iliad* I, 479–483, Richmond Lattimore translation.

Chapter 3
1. However, as a good Greek patriot he confessed to a *'frisson* of hate' on viewing the Elgin Marbles in the British Museum – Greek

classical treasures removed by Lord Elgin from the Acropolis in the early nineteenth century and never given back.

Chapter 5

1. Quoted in Fotakis, Z. *Greek Naval Strategy and Policy 1910–1919* (London and New York: Routledge 2005)

2. Despite the report of 'a heap of bodies', the Turkish casualty count was not as great as the Greeks believed; the sultan's navy probably suffered no more than fifteen men killed at Cape Helles and forty-one wounded.

Chapter 6

1. Barbara Tuchman, *The Guns Of August* (New York: Dell 1962) p. 161.

2. Hadjianestis, by all accounts, suffered from serious delusions, including the belief that his legs were made of glass and could shatter at any moment. Narrowly escaping execution was Prince Andrew of Greece, a sector commander and the father of the Duke of Edinburgh.

Chapter 8

1. According to Doxiadis who was on the bridge at the time, the reply was somewhat different: 'Faithful to duty and king, we are sailing to Souda ... Long live Greece!'

Chapter 9

1. At Port Said, the first stop, Captain Kondoyannis had ordered Iliomarkakis off the ship at gunpoint; the midshipman was later court-martialled and dishonourably discharged from the navy.

2. The *Exeter* was later sunk by the Japanese.

3. He would rejoin the RHN officer corps with the rank of commander in 1947 after a pardon, and retire the same year.
4. Happily, they got married and had two sons who grew up to be officers, one in the navy and the other in the air force. Imellos retired in 1967 with the rank of lieutenant commander.

Chapter 10
1. Arnold-Baker, R. and Cremos, G, *Averof: The Ship That Changed The Course Of History* (Athens: Akritas Publications 1990) p. 62.

Chapter 11
1. Blog by Vidos Kosmas on VimaPremium site, 31 December 2010.

Bibliographical Note

The only material available in English (apart from internet material of variable value) on the history of RHNS *Averof* is in the form of *Averof: The Ship that Changed the Course of History* by Richard Arnold-Baker and the late Commander George Cremos (Akritas Publications, 1990). Though the book contains the basic story and is largely accurate, it is lamentably brief and hence more of a museum publication than a serious history. Therefore I had to turn to much more abundant material in Greek.

The best source of information on the ship's record in the Balkan Wars is the memoir of Admiral Alexander Sakellariou, *An Admiral Remembers* (Yiota Sigma, undated). Sakellariou's eyewitness account of operations on board the *Averof*, from its commissioning until about the First World War, remains the best for that period. However, the memoir, though valuable for its descriptions and political insights, presents conspicuous gaps where Sakellariou skates vaguely over controversial points such as the decision in April 1941 to scuttle the armoured cruiser – a decision which was almost certainly his, though he may well have attempted to bury the issue in light of the crew's determination to keep it afloat and fighting.

The stories of officers and men serving on the *Averof* throughout the war are featured in a remarkable work of editing, the monumental five-volume *World War Two: The Warriors of the Navy Remember*, compiled painstakingly and with copious research notes by Vice

Admiral (ret.) Anastasios Dimitrakopoulos and published by the Hellenic Maritime Museum (2011). Though the work deals with the wartime history of the RHN as a whole as seen through its crewmembers' reminiscences, it throws a sharp and often disconcerting light on what was happening on board the *Averof* in those years. This, for example, has been the source for the startling narrative of Lieutenant Tsallis that takes up much of Chapter 8. More reminiscences, this time from the Balkan War era, are included in a small volume edited by Fotis Ladis, *Personal Diaries of Crewmembers of the Cruisers* Averof *and* Hydra, *1912–13* (Athens: Livanis 1993). Excerpts from the ship's log and technical records can be found in Nikos Stathakis, *George Averof: Chronicle of the Victory Cruiser.* Though published in 1987, it goes up only to 1948.

Material on the Ottoman Turkish navy of the first two decades of the twentieth century is not plentiful, but a general picture of the political and military situation of the Turks at the time is given by Bernard Lewis in his *The Emergence of Modern Turkey (Third Edition)* (Oxford University Press 2002). For a more general background on the development of armoured cruisers, a good source is Norman Friedman's excellent and highly detailed *British Cruisers of the Victorian Era* (Seaforth Publishers 2012). Though concentrating on the Royal Navy, Friedman gives enough information on European armoured cruisers to help a historian delve into the *Averof*'s parentage.

Index